INTRODUCTION

The Arrival Of The Red Settee

Following two successful pilot programmes, B̶ with Ali and Bernie sitting on the red leather Riverside goalmouth! It was an historic occa̶s̶i̶o̶n̶ ̶a̶n̶d̶ a technology coup as Middlesbrough beat giants Manchester United by six months to become the first football club to have their own television channel.

And what better pairing to front the programmes than the two men who had become local media celebrities for their exclusive and extremely popular Boro commentaries on Century Radio? Alastair Brownlee and Bernie Slaven.

But go back just a couple of years and the dedicated duo would have seemed the least likely candidates to end up doing the job. Just five years earlier Alastair had been regularly commentating on Boro games for BBC Radio Cleveland, while Bernie was in the business of banging in the goals for Boro. But Ali recalls: "If he'd had a bad game Slav would often sneak out the back way and avoid having to do press interviews." Not, one would think, the kind of behaviour you'd expect from a future TV presenter.

Ali's rise to local fame took an even stranger route. He was a part-time sports reporter at Radio Cleveland for 14 years as well as spending almost a quarter of a century dealing with money, money, money! No he wasn't a player too, but a bank manager!

So both men came into the media spotlight on the back of differing careers but it was a shared love of the Boro and their relationship as a pair that they point to as being the secrets of their success.

But what is the recipe for the perfect partnership?

ALI ON BERNIE

Ali, too, is forthright about their friendship, though he insists much of their success is down to his ability to wind Bernie up.

Ali says: "When Bernie first got involved in radio he wasn't anywhere near the personality he is now. We were thrown together in one of the most hectic times in Boro's history as we went on cup runs and tried to avoid relegation. We gelled and I think that was the making of us.

"He has his own opinions about football and the great thing is that as long as you disagree with him from time to time or vehemently put across another point of view, you can light the touch paper, sit back and watch the fireworks explode.

"My job is to try and keep the programme together so Bernie can go off on his tangents. And a Bernie Slaven who is excited, wants to throw verbal punches around and is up for a show, makes very, very good listening and viewing.

"On the way to Liverpool last season I told Bernie - falsely! - that there had been letters of complaint to Boro TV about his negative stance on the potential return of Juninho, and it could be the end of the road for us as a partnership. So he went to Anfield full of hell. We'd wound him up before he'd even started and we got a great commentary out of him.

He jokes: "It's essential that I'm with Bernie, even if I wasn't working on Boro TV, because I carry his ego so that he continues to be a Living Legend. I also keep him in crisps and chocolate. The night before we travel to distant away games I try to read up on Bernie's goalscoring record so I can inflate his ego by telling him what a great game he had against that side when he last played them."

"But, seriously, he is good fun and we do get on extremely well. He is a footballer through and through, though he used to say he didn't listen to my commentaries when I was working on the radio in the 1980s.

"However I've since found out that one day someone told him I'd been slagging him off on the radio. So he got one of his mates to record the commentary the following week to see what I was saying about him. Of course, he denies ever doing it!"

BERNIE ON ALI

People often ask if Ali and Bernie really get on with one another once the microphones and cameras are switched off. The truth, explains Bernie, is that the banter never stops and the pair have become close friends.

Bernie says: "Ali and I hit it off straight away. We are good friends off-set and our relationship has grown with Boro TV and Century. He's funny and bubbly and I like people like that. Sometimes he drives me mad with some of his comments about Boro, and this and that, but that's why it works so well.

"I think he sometimes pretends he's daft and says crazy things, like a certain player will score 60 goals that season when he knows full well he won't. But he wants me to pick up on that and give a response.

"I think Alastair is pro-Boro. Me I'm...honest! Some people like the fact that he's so biased and the same with my honesty, others don't. But I think we've got a happy medium and that's why we work so well together. We are both bubbly, hyper-active characters and we have a lot in common.

"Ali keeps me on my toes. If you sit watching a game as a fan with your mates there's a tendency not to concentrate as much and to flick through the programme or whatever. But now, because I don't know what questions Ali will fire at me next, I have to be aware and focused all the time, whether it's Boro TV or commentating on Century Radio.

"Ali has Boro in his blood and has been a supporter all his life. I'm also a Boro fan. I live here, my family lives here and I played for Boro, scored goals for Boro and was loyal to Boro, so I love them too.

"But there is one thing. Ali spends so much time at Hurworth that the only thing he doesn't join in with is training - and that's only because he's not fit enough!"

Boro TV kicks off

Following successful pilot shows the first ever Totally Red programme includes an interview with then Boro star Paul Merson in a feature series called "Bernie's About" that will see the former Boro striker interview the club's stars of the past and present in the months that follow. It takes place in Tall Trees Health Club in Yarm - and the magic man has a trick up his sleeve. The day also sees the start of a little bit of Boro TV action that will soon become a permanent fixture.

Ali explains: "Tall Trees Health Club was the obvious choice of place because that's where Bernie can often be seen displaying his hairy chest.

"We sat by the side of the swimming pool - with Bernie on the sunbed nearest the pool - when Merse whispered to me that he was going to push the Living Legend into the water halfway through the interview. Bernie was oblivious to this and Merse carried on with the questions as we waited. But, at the last minute, the Magic Man changed his mind because he didn't know what would have happened had Bernie gone in with a live microphone in his hand. We nearly had fried Slaven on our hands!

"Also that day, Bernie got the idea of catching the microphone at the start of "Bernie's About". As we walked out of Tall Trees, there was a colourful car promoting one of their '70s nights and Bernie said; 'Just throw me the mike and I'll do a preview for next week'. But he kept dropping the damn thing! Eventually, after several takes, we taught him how to catch and the flying mike soon became a regular thing."

Bernie admits: *"I didn't know anything about the plans to push me in the pool until months later when Ali spilled the beans. If I had gone in I'd have laughed because I'm a bit of a prankster myself and I could relate to that. But I'd have made sure I threw the wet mike in the direction of Merse before I went under."*

And he insists that catching the mike was actually the idea of one of the Boro production team.

"We actually stopped doing it after a couple of weeks but we received letters from people saying they liked it so it returned and became something of a trademark. The problem is I'm still not very good at catching the bloody thing!"

9 July

Boro New Boys

Boro unveil new signings Gary Pallister and Dean Gordon to the nation at a press conference at the club. Bernie is to be reunited with his best mate Pally, and the Boro TV team get their chance to interview the club's latest stars. But is there something bigger ready to break?

Ali: "All of Teesside seemed to be expecting Robbo to announce that as well as Dean Gordon and Gary Pallister a further star was to be signed, having been used to the likes of Juninho and Ravanelli arriving.

"In fact, when we arrived at the stadium for the press conference, one of the cleaning ladies insisted that Juninho was there and that Robbo had put him in one of the executive boxes. When I denied the rumour she took away the coffee and tea from our room in disgust!

"Bernie was reunited with his old mate, Gary Pallister. He had gone on record to say that he wouldn't pay any more than £500,000 for Pally, so the size of the £2.5m fee surprised the Living Legend. So much so that when Bernie was due at the stadium to interview Pally he drove to the training ground by mistake and kept Pally waiting half an hour."

Bernie: "I am big mates with Pally from our days at Boro together and never lost touch with him during his time at Man United. When I moved to Port Vale I didn't live too far from him so I used to see him a lot and took in quite a few United games - although I can't recall him coming to watch any at Port Vale! When he told me in the summer that he was possibly coming back, well before the deal was struck, I told him that if I was signing him I'd pay £500,000. When he told me United were asking £2.5million, I thought he was joking. It is like buying an old car - although Pally would say 'vintage'.

"But, seriously, I was delighted that he came back, not only because he is a mate but because he is the most successful player in Manchester United's history."

Rumours of another new signing prove to be unfounded but the Boro TV team pride themselves on the fact that they are well placed to cover any eventuality.

Ali: "The beauty of Boro TV is that, being a small team, we can react to events as we would have been able to had something else happened at the press conference. For the BBC or whoever to do an outside broadcast they may have had to get in extra cameramen or producers but we can literally say 'there's our cameraman and producer - let's do it'. We can react very quickly."

The press conference also gives the team a chance to see manager Bryan Robson - a key participant in Boro TV - after his and the players' summer breaks.

Ali: "I think Robbo is absolutely brilliant for Boro TV. He does a feature called "Robbo Replies" in which the fans put questions directly to him and he previews the game coming up. He's always happy to do it and appreciates that the fans are the lifeblood of the club.

"Without the boss the show wouldn't be half as good. He even refers to Boro TV as his own television station. During the season, MUTV was launched and they kept asking him for interviews, but he took great delight in shouting 'tell them to **** off, I have my own TV station'."

Bernie: "It's important to keep in touch with everyone at the club and not to lose touch. Boro TV is not all about me and Ali - it's about Middlesbrough Football Club. It's important the punters get to see a general picture of what's happening at the club they love."

10 July

Bernie Back Home

The popular feature "Bernie's About" sees the living legend travel all over the place for a chat with former Boro greats as well as present stars. On this occasion the interviewee is ex-midfielder Bobby Murdoch. The visit to Glasgow also gives Bernie the chance to return to his roots.

Ali: "Bernie's About had already become a huge hit over the summer and we had done some very entertaining features. I'll always remember the one we did at the time groundsman David Rigg was re-laying the pitch at the stadium. Club Public Relations Manager Dave Allan came along to give us an update and we decided to do it from a dodgy looking caravan parked up at the side of the pitch. So he climbed inside the caravan but then minor disaster struck. Firstly, the door locked from the outside and he couldn't get out, and, secondly, there was a bloke snoring inside. We had to open the door and get Dave out of there as quickly as possible. We never did find out who it was inside!"

For another "Bernie's About", Bernie travelled back to his birthplace in Glasgow.

"We found ourselves travelling to Glasgow with Slav endlessly reciting the Lisbon Lions (Glasgow Celtic) feats of glory," smiles Ali. "He also said he knew Glasgow like the back of his hand from his days there.

"Bobby Murdoch was a true football great and even at the end of his career, as his waistline expanded to match his silverware cabinet, he was a key influence in Jack Charlton's Boro promotion side of the mid-1970s. He would be a millionaire in today's game so it was a bit of a shame to see him living in a council house in Glasgow struggling to get a ticket to see the team he once starred for. His financial restraints meant that he remains to this day the only person to ask for a fee for a Boro TV interview, but he was a great guest guiding us around Celtic Park and showing us the dressing rooms and trophies which mark a great past.

"Following the interview we decided to go on a tour of Glasgow - Slav immediately directed us the wrong way down a one-way street. So much for the back of his hand!"

Bernie: *"I get a choice of where I want to go and who I want to interview when it comes to "Bernie's About". So when Bobby's name came up I thought 'great' because he is not only a hero of mine, but it also took me back home. His house was about five minutes from my parents' and travelling up there I was excited about seeing the great Bobby Murdoch. When we got there he took us to see the trophy room at the mighty Parkhead and he was so proud to show us around. He was a great host and a great man. What did upset me was to see a man of his talents living in a council house after such a glittering career. I mean there are guys around now who aren't even good enough to lace his boots playing the game and earning a lot of money."*

12 July

Anyone for cricket?

A rainy Sunday afternoon sees Boro TV head in the direction of Saltburn Cricket Club along with most of Boro's first team squad (enjoying their last day of freedom before pre-season training starts) who are taking part in a charity match for the Jamie Hood Appeal. It is the sort of thing Boro TV are keen to get involved with and on this occasion it is very close to Ali's heart.

He explains: "Jamie was a promising cricketer who went to play in South Africa only to be seriously hurt in a car crash. The cricket team who took Jamie abroad forgot the essential matter of insurance and left Jamie's Mam and Dad with a huge financial burden to help their paralysed son.

"When I worked for Barclays Bank in Redcar I got to know the Hoods and was more than delighted to take the Boro TV cameras along to support the cause. A day nearly ruined by rain ended up a success and the players who turned up seemed to enjoy their last drink of freedom before returning to training."

13 July

Back to work

The players arrive back for pre-season training, as do the Boro TV cameras. Gazza and Paul Merson arrive along with the rest of the lads but Merse is very fit after being at the World Cup and he is given permission to go off on a family holiday to America. Andy Townsend is revealed as the new club captain on a day when an attempt at a new angle goes a little awry.

Ali: "It was like something out of The Italian Job. Our cameraman, Alex, set up his camera on the back of the groundsman Arthur's buggy and set off after the players for a moving shot of the lads jogging.

"Alex's eye for the girls ensured two more passengers - both female. However, Arthur, instead of keeping a discreet distance, set off rapidly towards the training pitches - and the players - with a cart full of people and a camera. The players started to realise Arthur was coming towards them at about 90mph. Viv Anderson told the lads to stop what they were doing and sit on the floor as Arthur did a handbrake turn and screamed to a standstill inches from the edge of the pitch. Everyone was in shock at what they had just seen but Arthur just turned round and said 'there they are, there's the players'. It was the classic example of how important it is to brief EVERYONE on exactly what you are doing before you start filming."

Bernie: *"It was important to be at pre-season training to show people who think life as a footballer is a bed of roses that that's not the case. It's not just about scoring goals and being on TV, there is a lot of hard slog. I was just happy I was only talking and not running!*

"Pre-season is the worst time for a professional player because you've just come back from a refreshing break and for two weeks solid you just run your socks off. I have seen players be physically sick because of the

amount of exercise they've had to do. It's just like going back to school. You've had seven weeks off and you're a bit nervous on the night before going back. You're delighted in one sense because you're going back to see your mates but on the other hand you know you are there to work."

15 July

£300 on the nose

A visit to the training ground to interview Robbie Mustoe ends in Bernie meeting up with Gazza's infamous mate, Jimmy 'Five Bellies' Gardner. He sees Jimmy has a painful looking wound on the bridge of his nose and, being the intrepid Boro TV presenter that he is, decides to investigate.

Bernie: "I couldn't believe it when I saw Jimmy. He had a cut on his nose about the size of a 10p coin. When he told me he'd held a lighter to his nose for a £300 bet Gazza had set him I was gobsmacked. It looked like he had three nostrils. I mean, as I've said before, I'm a bit of a prankster but even I wouldn't go that far.

"I had to laugh. Then a couple of weeks later I saw him again and it didn't seem to be getting any better. I stopped to chat to him and he told me he'd done it again for another bet!"

20 July

The Wolfman gets wet

Ex-Boro 'keeper turned goalkeeping coach Stephen Pears is the subject for Boro TV's interview on a wet and rainy occasion but, as is always the case, the intrepid pair Ali and Bernie are determined to surround the chat with the very best footage. And it doesn't turn out bad - although it is a rare opportunity to call Mr Slaven a "drip".

Bernie: "Ali came up with the idea of me taking a few shots at Pearsy on camera before I had my chat with him. But when we went to see if there was any kit available we were told there wasn't. Our plan looked scuppered. Then my good friend Pally came in from training and said he had some I could borrow - but it had to be the stuff he had on! So I went out in his wet, smelly gear all for the love of Boro TV - that's what friends are for!"

That evening Bernie attends the launch of former Boro player

and manager Willie Maddren's autobiography, Extra Time. Willie, who was a key part of Jack Charlton's 1973-74 Division Two championship winning side, later took charge of the side and Bernie was his very last signing. Tragically, Willie now suffers from the debilitating illness Motor Neurone Disease and his book is helping to raise money for research into the disease.

Bernie: "I've got a lot to thank Willie for. He brought me to Middlesbrough and for that I'll be eternally grateful. They say in life that all the good guys get problems and Willie is certainly a good guy. He was great as a manager, perhaps too nice, and was an all-round gentlemen. It's tragic for a man like Willie, who never did anybody any harm, to get MND. I went along to the event for two reasons. Firstly because Willie is my friend and I owe him a lot but secondly to support the MND Fund. After seeing what Willie has gone through the charity is something I will continue to support. It makes me realise how lucky I am."

21 July

The Italian Job

The Boro TV team interview Italian pair Gianluca Festa and Marco Branca. They decide to take them to Sardi's Italian restaurant in Darlington, to give the feature the perfect setting and to make the players feel comfortable in their surroundings. Everything goes extremely well and a very similar shoot later appears on Sky - a compliment to Boro TV.

Ali: "The duo were great hosts. Branca was in high spirits because he was very optimistic about the season ahead but his knee seemed to be troubling him and, with his goalscoring ability needed in the Premiership, that was the only concern over pasta.

"Everyone knows Festa has restored Teesside's faith in Italians after the sour taste of Ravanelli. Luca was surprised to be so popular. Evidently in Serie A defenders receive few accolades. His only gripe was that it was a little different in Darlington than in Sardinia - which is probably a fair point!

"They were great together - the Italian Laurel and Hardy. At that stage, Marco was staying at Luca's house and the rest of the Festa family were still in Italy. I could just imagine a sink full of dirty pots after a botched attempt at making tagliatelle."

Bernie: *"Ali always gets to go to the glamorous restaurants to do his interviews whereas I usually have to sit on a park bench with a bag of fish and chips. Then again, look what good the rich food has done him!"*

22 July

Who us?

A complaint is made to Boro chiefs about Boro TV filming in the players' canteen at Hurworth. Wires have been crossed somewhere along the line as it was in fact a rival station who had been in the eating area. A new system is soon put in place to allow Boro TV to eat there also - but for now a Big Mac will have to do.

Ali: "A complaint was made about filming in the players' restaurant and although we were innocent we copped the blame. We are careful not to be in the lads' faces and it seemed as though someone was out to make a bit of mischief at our expense. I stressed to the club that we have no intention of ever filming players eating and made a mental note to ensure that the cameras are not even stored in the eating area. I was told that we'd have to collect a pass to eat, only then to be told that the passes hadn't been printed yet. It was back to McDonald's at Darlington again!"

Grouchy Gordon

The same day Alastair arranges a chat with Gordon McQueen about his appointment as first team coach. But events from a little earlier on had left Mr McQueen just a little grouchy to begin with.

Ali: "Initially Gordon's mood was a little dour as, apparently, Viv arranged for sandwiches at lunch but, somehow, forgot to pay, leaving Gordon with the bill. You know a Scot and his money!

"Gordon has all the attributes to be a great coach - a vast knowledge of the game from a career with Leeds, Man United and Scotland as well as the physique to scare the s**t out of anyone who dares to cross him. Boro TV-wise, Gordon is great. For a spell he worked for Sky and he comes across really well and knows exactly what is needed by the camera crew."

Off to Dublin - or are we?

While Ali is busy chatting to Gordon McQueen, Bernie is equally as occupied trying to set up a trip to Glasgow with Curtis Fleming and Alan Moore to see St Patrick's play a friendly against Celtic. Bernie is desperate to see his Glaswegian idols in action again and it will also be a special occasion for Curtis as St Patrick's are his former club. But, at the last minute, things go a little bit wrong.

Bernie: *"I had done an interview at Blackwell Grange hotel in Darlington and Curtis had arranged to pick me up from there. Ali waited with me until Curtis turned up and I was really looking forward to the game. However, when Curtis arrived he told me that his kid was poorly and that we couldn't go. I was a bit disappointed but I understood the reasons why and rang my dad in Scotland to tell him there were four spare tickets for the game. The only thing was, the tickets were with a chap we knew who was waiting at Parkhead - and my dad had never met him before in his life. Apparently, by the time found him it was almost half-time!"*

23 July

Merse goes missing

The Boro TV set - featuring the leather settee and surrounded by all sorts of Boro memorabilia - has become almost as familiar and popular as the two men presenting the programmes. When Paul Merson was a Middlesbrough player, a cardboard cut-out of him took pride of place in the corner - but after a loan spell at a Boro Book Fair he almost went missing forever.

Ali: "When we started Boro TV the Magic Man was very much a hero figure and we had the cut-out. On this day we lent it to the club and promised to pick it up later. But when we went back no-one knew where it had gone and even a search of every room and executive box failed to find Merse. At this point we were thinking we'd have to do the programme without it until a little bird told us that the cleaning ladies had taken it into their room. I expected them to have set up a shrine to him in the corner of their room but no, instead they had thrown him in the skip. We rescued him but I couldn't help thinking that it might be an omen."

Bernie: *"At the time, Merse was a big name and when we first started out the cardboard figure was the first thing people saw when they tuned in to the programme. It was certainly better looking than either me or Ali.*

"I remember being a little embarrassed when I interviewed Merse and I started asking him about his nickname Magic Man. I just presumed it was something to do with his skills but seemingly it originated from his days at Arsenal and was actually connected with his then drinking habits!"

24 July

Ali in hospital

Alastair spends a Friday evening on South Cleveland Hospital Radio giving patients a two hour chat about Boro TV and Century Radio commentaries. Both he and Bernie have been lucky enough to work their way up the media ladder and that is why Boro TV pledged their support.

Ali: "I went along for two hours and discussed all sorts of things about TV and radio as well as answering questions. It was also a good way of giving something back to those in hospital having a bit of a miserable time. One Boro-mad bloke rang up and said he listened to all my commentaries and watched Boro TV. He was gutted because he couldn't escape the sound of my voice even when he was in hospital!"

Bernie: *"It was great that Ali went along to the hospital and told them all about what we do. It can only help boost people's awareness of Boro TV. But maybe they should have kept him in a while longer. After some of the comments I've heard him say about Boro over the years I'm sure there's a bed in the psychiatric ward with his name on it."*

25 July

Football is back

Hednesford are Boro's opponents in the first pre-season friendly of 1998. The game brings back memories of a fantastic FA Cup game at the Riverside when the conference side nearly knocked a Juninho, Emerson and Ravanelli-filled Boro out of the FA Cup. On that occasion Boro struggled to a 3-2 win but all the praise, rightly so, was poured on the heads of the Hednesford players.

The non-league side had billed the friendly as a 'Gazza-game' to sell as many tickets as possible but neither Gascoigne nor Merson featured. The game ends in a drab 0-0 draw and the events of half-time are perhaps more interesting than anything else!

Ali: "The game was billed as Gazza's comeback after his England disappointment but it turned out neither Gazza nor Merse would feature. The large crowd was disappointed by the star names' absence and a tame 0-0 draw was a low key start.

"However, a couple whose wedding reception was booked at the ground had their pictures taken with Robbo at half time to the great delight of the fans. When the teams ran back out they were still on the pitch taking photos which everyone found amusing."

26 July

Hot stuff

The hectic pre-season build up is starting to take its toll on the Living Legend and he heads to the sauna at the Tall Trees Health Club with his mate Gary Pallister. The venue would become a popular one for the pair over the coming season.

Bernie: *"We are great mates. Pally's the kind of guy who, no matter how much success he has, is not a big mouth and hasn't got an ego. When we go out together we talk about everything else but football and that's great because we both spend all day, every day working in the game. I think it's important to get away from the football and everything that goes with it every now and again and I reckon nothing beats a sauna. I often spend a lot of time in front of a camera and, although I enjoy the work, it's often hot and sweaty - so for something different I have a sauna!"*

27 July

Off to Stockport

A dramatic start to the week as Peter Wilcock, ntl's Director of Sales and Marketing, returns from holiday. He feels a change of cameraman is the order of the day and the new man to come in is Simon Hanning who delights Bernie with tales of his friendship with Robbie Williams. Slav in return, introduces him

to the delights of the Tall Trees and Simon wakes up with one hell of a hangover.

Ali: "Sadly, cameraman Alex moved on and I was pleased he got a job with Sky. Alex is good at his job and will survive but the first member of the original team had left so it did leave a bit of a funny feeling."

But the team need to quickly get over any shock as they head off for another pre-season friendly at Stockport and a chance for Ali and Bernie to go back to a few old haunts as well as seeing the likes of Gazza and Gary Pallister in action.

Ali: "Two seasons earlier Bernie and I had done our first solo Century commentary at Stockport in the Coca Cola Cup semi-final. We had come a long way since then but some still wonder why I gave up a safe job with Barclays Bank to do Boro TV and Century Radio.

"Bernie again claimed he knew somewhere else like the back of his hand (Stockport) and we decided to go back to the same chippy we'd been to the last time. But then the Living Legend got us sucked into the Stockport one-way system and we headed off in the direction of Preston. By the time we eventually found the chippy we were absolutely starving. But our good old fashioned eatery had changed hands and become an Indian takeaway so we didn't bother after all that."

Bernie: *"It was great to see Pally playing again but I was a little surprised as I thought he'd still be knackered from pre-season training! But he did make an appearance and played well.*

"The trip to Stockport actually brought back memories of the last time Ali and I went there for a match. It was in the days before Ali had his sponsored car and we travelled there in his old banger. I was suffering from a bout of sciatica in my back at the time and I needed to get some warmth through my body but the heating wasn't working in the car and I was absolutely freezing. I also needed to stretch to ease the pain so I spent the entire journey with the window down and my legs hanging out of the window."

28 July

Give us Moore

Young Irish forward Alan Moore isn't one for giving interviews and hadn't ever faced the cameras before Boro TV spoke exclusively to him. But what could have become a damp squib in

fact turns into one of the most enlightening and interesting Boro TV interviews to date.

Ali: "Moorsey is a genuinely likeable, quiet lad who has struggled with injury problems and a lack of form. In the past, fans had talked about Alan being the new Wilf Mannion or the new Ryan Giggs and Liverpool were, it was said, preparing a million pound bid - then came his injuries and loss of form.

"He hadn't given any interviews before but spoke well of his injury problems. The circulation in his legs had become so difficult the previous year that he couldn't feel his feet after games. An operation to his veins was so complex that only one leg could receive surgery at a time and the season had all but been written off. Fans don't see the pain barrier that players go through and the way that not playing tears at a player's soul. The interview gave them an insight. But a new season was dawning and Moorsey felt fit. Oh, and could his mam have a copy of the interview!"

29 July

Merson memories

A year before this pre-season friendly at York, Alastair had first met the Magic Man as a Boro player, again at a pre-season game and again at York. At the time, Merse was a little uncertain as he was about to start his first season outside the top flight since an early career loan spell at Brentford. He would also be Ali's first ever Boro TV interviewee.

Twelve months later and Merse and co are playing their last warm-up game before another crack at the Premiership - but it is Colombian striker Hamilton Ricard, who had had a slow start in a Boro shirt, who is grabbing the headlines.

Ali: "Pally was still finding his feet and picked up a knock against York which would disrupt his start to the season, but that was the only downside to the game. Hamilton Ricard scored a late goal and if he had heard some of the fans' criticism he did not show it.

"Ricard looked to have all the makings of a class centre forward - a Colombian international with great physique and a good touch. It's just that when he arrived from Deportivo Cali, as Bernie put it, 'He couldn't hit a cows bum with a banjo'. But with Branca injured and Armstrong out we were hoping he would learn to strum the banjo."

Bernie: *"The banjo saying definitely belongs to Ali. I'm more likely to have said that he couldn't hit a barn door. But if I ever did say that I would only have been joking because I don't believe in slating individuals.*

"Hamilton had been having a bad time but I think the York game was a bit of a turnaround for him. Every striker has a bad patch - I've been there - and the only way to make yourself and the punters happy is to score a goal. Although it was only a pre-season game you could see him growing in confidence."

30 July

Ali and Bob - not Vic and Bob

As Boro TV grows, so does its range of programmes and Century Radio's Bob Moncur Football Phone-In, featuring Ali alongside the former Newcastle star, sees its way on to Boro TV screens.

But when the show comes back on air after a summer break, there is an essential part of it missing - Bob Moncur!

Ali: "We started the programme again and I was really excited that Bob and I would be in the same studio instead of him in Newcastle and me in Middlesbrough. But someone forgot to tell Bob. Cue panic at 5.45pm (the show starts at 6pm) when there was no sign of him. Then news came through that he was sailing on the high seas in his yacht - which I call the Black Pig, after Captain Pugwash."

1-2 August

Sheer four team boredom - The JD Sports Cup

It was to have been Boro, Fiorentina, Benfica and the Mags...a weekend of Merse, Gazza, Shearer and Batistuta live on Sky. Instead, Fiorentina are replaced by Italian minnows Empoli and Ali and Bernie - this time in their capacity as Century Radio commentators - begin to feel the whole weekend going pear-shaped.

Ali: "The corners at the stadium were nearing completion but you couldn't help feeling the workers could have done without an enforced weekend break. David Rigg, the groundsman, had also worked all summer in re-seeding the pitch and presumably he could also have done without the tournament.

"The games were all live on Century, which caused a few moments of humour as Slav failed to pronounce any foreign player's name correctly and refused to talk about any team other than the Boro.

"It reminded me of when the Chinese national team played Boro at Ayresome Park and the PA announcer - I think it was Bernard Gent - gave out the Boro side...tried, coughed and spluttered over the first name in the opposition line up and then said, to huge cheers, 'China are as per the programme..'

"To add insult to injury the football was dire and both Boro and Newcastle lost on day one. It was left to Benfica and Empoli to stretch patience thin by taking the final to penalties. I began to think it could be a long season."

Bernie: *"Probably the most entertaining moment of the whole tournament came when Ali inadvertently gave out the nickname of Rachel Whatley, our head of sport, on air. We were trying to attract her attention at pitchside and couldn't get through to her so he shouted "Rampant, what's going on?" To his embarrassment he later found out his words had reached the ears of all the Century listeners."*

3 August

Welcome on board

Boro TV has a new cameraman called Graeme Fisher who hails from 'down south', much to the pleasure of Ali, who immediately gets on the mickey-taking bandwagon.

Bernie: "Graeme arrived and Ali discovered he was a Chelsea fan so straight away he gave him the mindstretching nickname of "cockers" - which seems to have stuck. It's short for cockney and it's all we ever call him these days."

6 August

Double Dutch

Bernie's well documented fear of flying is put to the test on a three-day tour of Holland which sees Boro take on Heerenveen and hosts Den Haag. Alastair and a Boro TV editor/cameraman, Rob King, fly out with the Boro squad but poor old Bernie faces an 18-hour journey as he joins the supporters on their coach. A great time is had by all but Bernie's phobia is put to the test on the way home - will he or won't he fly?

Bernie: "Ali had booked me on the flight with the players but my nerves once again got the better of me, so instead I arranged for a place on the supporters' coach. I wasn't officially booked on the coach so I had to sit in the spare driver's seat at the front. It was a bit uncomfortable so when we got halfway down the A19 I asked the driver if there was a bed and, to my surprise, he replied 'It's below you'. So I crawled into the coffin-like bunker and fell asleep as soon as my head hit the bunker. Some of the fans later said they couldn't get to sleep up above because of the noise of my snoring. I awoke to the smell of seaside air as we arrived in Dover and then we set off for Calais. The ferry ride was smooth as it was a lovely day."

Ali: "Bernie left Rob and I to record the team's departure from Teesside Airport, and, of course, make the flight. On the short flight, I sat next to Curtis Fleming. I will always remember that he gave us one of the best interviews on Boro TV when he recalled a thunder storm which broke when he was in the house with his two young daughters. He heard a bang and thought 'my god I know I haven't been playing well but the fans are blowing up the car', and then the TV blew up and the sockets flew out of the wall - , apparently, it was like a scene from The Exorcist.' It was the result of a direct hit from lightening.

"'Flash' has great respect on Teesside for trying patiently and with diplomatic care to explain to Ravanelli that he was out of order...in other words he chinned him! If only that had been done sooner...

"Travelling with the team had a few unwritten rules which were observed by Eric Paylor of the Evening Gazette and I. The lads don't want to feel as if they are being asked for interviews or being reported on all the time. Because of this I made a request via the club's PR department to have a chat with Merse at some stage, speak with Bryan after the games and record the matches and training.

"On arrival, we had a brief moment of financial drama. Normally on trips where the press accompany the official party the bill is sent to the club and they then forward it to the individual members of the press for settlement, but something strange was in the air as Eric and I were told we had to pay there and then. Thankfully, Barclaycard came to my rescue for Rob, Bernie and I but Eric had only a piece of plastic which would struggle to gain recognition on Linthorpe Road - I offered to stick his bill on my now seriously threatened credit limit, but after a body search which would have done HM Customs justice, Eric was able to pay. Incidentally, at the time of writing the hotel are trying to get us to pay again!"

After sorting out the initial problems Ali and co. set about working out their agenda for the next few days. The matches are on the Friday (August 7) and Sunday (August 9) so they work out that the Saturday night will offer them the best opportunity to see the sights of Amsterdam. However, Paul Merson is to put a further dampener on matters by refusing to do an interview for Boro TV. Calling captain Andy Townsend to the rescue!

Ali: "After our evening meal I attended a formal reception for the Middlesbrough team held in the hotel and on the way I mentioned to Merse my hope for an interview for Boro TV at a time to suit him, only to receive a cold 'Sorry, no interviews for anyone'. Andy T came over and asked what was up and said 'Look Al, will I do...Merse may not be up to it'. As always, it was Andy to the rescue but I did admit to feelings of frustration as Eric Paylor also got the same reaction from Merse. We were the local media for heaven's sake, no one was going to stitch him up.

"The only people to watch Boro TV were the people who hero worshipped him and paid his wages. It's at times like that, thankfully rare over the years, that I would love to say on radio or TV 'look we wanted to interview X but basically he cannot be bothered' and then see what reception he would get at the next match. The reception was a low-key affair. Robbo, as always, was the perfect diplomat but with Merse in a mood he left and soon the organisers drew the evening to an early close."

Merse sees red

The first game of the Dutch weekend sees Boro get off to the worst possible start but at least Ali is reunited with his sparring partner Bernie who has survived the mammoth coach journey and arrived in Holland in one piece.

Ali: "The evening game with Heerenven at the Den Haag Stadium did little to allay fears as the referee sent off Merse for a late challenge and Boro fell away to defeat. Robbo was furious after the game and the coach back to the hotel was subdued, but at least Slav was on board. The Living Legend had arrived after a marathon 18 hours on the Supporters Club coach and was walking like Max Wall but he was here and declaring that he would be flying home. 'We shall see', I thought. He had boarded the coach at the Riverside, found the spare driver's sleeping bunk, thrown his kit on it and survived on chocolate and telling the fans about how he scored his Boro goals for the full journey. The fans looked as relieved as Slav that the torture was all over!

"We got back to our hotel and within seconds our room was a mess. Bernie was trimming his chest hair with my shaver and keen for a night out... 'Dinnae trouble the lads, they will be too upset for interviews. Now, where's the beach and nightclubs?' We returned later to a strange smelling room. Slav's wife had packed a tuna pasta before he left. But 18 hours in a coach and the heat of the Hague had worked a certain magic. Slav noticed that Alan Moore had left his door open and deposited the tuna there. 'Moorsey won't mind, all the Irish stick together,' was his reasoning."

Bernie: "I met up with Ali at the stadium in Den Haag but he seemed a little surprised to see me. He said he had had his doubts as to whether I would turn up, but I had kept my promise and, after all, Boro TV is my job.

"The game against Heerenveen was average to say the least. From the Boro fans point of view it was spoilt by the sending off of their hero Merse and we were all just hoping the remaining game of the tour would be much better.

"Later that night myself, Ali and Eric Paylor went back to our hotel and then for a walk along the seafront. We met up with Boro's chief scout Ron Bone and he invited us into the company of Viv Anderson back at the hotel. We had a great time having a drink and talking about every aspect of football until the early hours. We all said our goodbyes and then sloped off to bed although I'm sure the others were a bit more knackered than me - I'd spent the last 18 hours asleep on the coach!"

8 August

Amsterdam by night - Andy Townsend by day

The heat is searing in Scheveningen and Bernie and Ali are looking forward to a day without a match and a chance to see the sights. But before they can do this there is the small matter of an interview with Andy Townsend. But where is he?

Ali: "Scheveningen is like Torremolinos, and the weather was superb. It seemed like all of Holland was heading for the beaches and I just couldn't help thinking 'Why am I in the hotel?' Andy had agreed to do the Boro TV interview with Bernie and I at 2pm, giving us plenty of time to change and then head with Eric Paylor to Amsterdam. However two-o-clock turned into 2-30pm, then 3pm, and Bernie's mood darkened. It became positively thunderlike when he was informed that the players were at a bar over the road enjoying a few drinks.

"Slav believes that if an interview is set for a certain time then, within reason, that time should be kept, but sometimes reporting on any football team is a matter of diplomacy. We are after all paid to do Boro TV so it makes little sense falling out with people you have to work with during the season. I also remember trying to interview the Living Legend when he was a player. After scoring a goal or having a good game he would slam open the players entrance door and demand his press corps attended to him, but after a defeat it was a dash through the back door to the car park, leaving a trail of journalists in his wake. The boot is now firmly on the other foot. Slav left at 3.30pm, Andy arrived at 4pm, apologised and did a great interview. He felt that when you looked at the playing strength of Southampton, Coventry, Charlton, Forest and many others you wouldn't swop their players for ours and if we got off to a good start in the coming season we would be fine.

"Now, to find Bernie, and on to Amsterdam. On the train from the Hague, Slav was disturbed to find out that Amsterdam was hosting the gay Olympics but recovered to entertain some girls with a fine array of farmyard noises until told by a lady passenger to shut up. The Legend recovered composure to invite the woman to join us, which she did, only to show a document stating she has been deported from the UK. She was on her way back to Slovakia and we bought her dinner before being guided to the red light district.

"After a great night out, we enjoyed chatting to Viv (or should that be Bernie raging about tactics) about the need to buy and playing formations. Slav stated that as long as we stayed up it did not matter if we packed the defence, played five at the back and had a season of stability. Viv believed that Robbo would always pick a side with flair, even if it meant being threatened with relegation. He said the boss would rather walk away than give up his principles about the way the game should be played. Viv noticed that Robbo had arrived at the bar and was standing behind Slav and said 'I bet you wouldn't say any of these things in front of the boss.' Slav bit back 'I'm not frightened of him, I scored a few past him when he was at United' to which Viv replied 'Good, tell him he's just behind you!'

"Back to the room and surprise, the tuna pasta was back - but this time it was under Slav's pillow. And Merse had checked out and left for home."

Bernie: *"On the Saturday, 2.30pm came around and Andy Townsend still hadn't arrived to do the interview, so I told Ali I wasn't sitting around waiting while the weather was so great outside. I went for a walk along the beach. I saw some of the lads sitting in a cafe enjoying a break - and to my dismay Andy Townsend was there. So I went back and told Ali he was wasting his time, but he decided to carry on waiting for him.*

"Eventually we got to travel to Amsterdam and the famous red light district. We jumped on a tram but it was absolutely jam packed - with Ali's backside taking up most of the space. We sat opposite two young Dutch girls, who looked like they were about 16, and I asked them if they spoke English and they nodded slightly. The charm started to flow and I told them we'd been there for days and that I'd not yet seen a windmill or a pair of clogs. Then for a laugh I had them doing animal noises like pigs, cows, sheeps and ducks. Everyone else on the tram must have thought we were bonkers.

"We went to the red light district - what an education - and it wasn't seedy at all! I saw a fantastic fountain that would look great in my back garden."

9 August

Ham the man

Boro produce a win in Holland and it's Hamilton Ricard who is the star with a stunning goal. But the nerves are starting to set in for Bernie as he's just hours away from facing his biggest fear - FLYING HOME!

Ali: "Although Boro suffered a few setbacks in Holland the Boro fans had a fantastic weekend conquering Amsterdam and taking in the sunshine. They even indulged in a 30-a-side kick about behind the stadium before the kick off. The police joined in but, sadly, Bernie didn't, blaming an old back injury.

"The real match brought a 3-2 win for Boro and Hamilton Ricard scored with a spectacular chip from 20 yards. Maybe the journey home was a little easier for Gordon McQueen and scout Ray Train as they had recommended Ricard. In reality, Gordon's judgement is without question as I remember he said to me early in the year: 'The best full back in the club is Robbie Stockdale, he will be some player.' Without adding to any pressure on Robbie he is the most mature teenager I have come across, he is very comfortable with the media, in fact I'm thinking about asking him to be a more regular contributor to Boro TV and I know it would not faze him. I first met Robbie when I was working with Barclays and visited Bydales School in Marske on a regular basis to help the Business Studies department. Robbie was a pupil at the school, well regarded by the teachers and very level headed and he gave the impression of someone who knew exactly what his future was to hold.

"On the coach going to the game Robbo was blowing a gasket. Gustavo Lombardi, an Argentinean full-back on loan until the end of the year and desperate to impress, was not allowed to play. Lombardi had played for the Argentinean national side and would have been in the squad for France 98 had injury not intervened. 'I might have marked Michael Owen and stopped him scoring that goal,' he joked to me. But no one was laughing that day as his administration forms had not come through and he was not eligible to play."

Bernie: "The game against hosts Den Haag was a definite improvement on the first match and it put a smile on the faces of all the Boro fans who had enjoyed a cracking weekend in Holland. It was great to see Hamilton get off the mark in such style. It was a cracking finish and one that did him no end of good in terms of confidence. On the worrying side of things, as the day went by I had to decide whether or not I was facing my fear and flying home - but when the supporters' coach left for England straight after the game my mind was made up for me...I would have to fly."

10 August

Bernie and his tortoise

The day of reckoning has arrived as Bernie confronts his phobia and attempts to get on a plane for the first time in years. It is to

be a momentous day as the Living Legend conquers his fear - albeit with a little bit of help. But it is Ali and friends who have the last laugh.

Ali: "Bernie had to face his nemesis - the flight home. He had been given some valium earlier in the year when he was due to coach in the USA with Mark Proctor but his fear overcame him and Proc was dispatched to the States on his own. A few months later further valium was added when Slav was invited by Boro chairman Steve Gibson to Cyprus for a tournament, but he decided that Glasgow was a better option.

"So the Slav, full of valium once more, nervously headed for the coach carrying a box containing a lamp purchased in Holland on the side of which I had written in large letters TORTOISE!

"On boarding the coach Robbo asked if Slav was OK and in an attempt to make conversation said 'What's in the box?' Slav looked at the letters and replied in slow speech 'A tortoise, have you got a lettuce leaf?' Robbo retreated with a bemused look on his face. To his immense credit Slav made it home, but to add rich irony, his luggage was left in Holland. 'Typical Slav' said Andy Townsened, 'Even the Dutch thought you wouldn't make the flight...they kept your case as they thought you would go back and get the bus!'

Bernie: *"I woke up that morning very nervous and after doing a piece for the cameras on the seafront I went back to the hotel for a breakfast made specially to prepare nerves - valium! I had bought a Chinese lamp the day before and it was in a big box ready to carry home. Ali had written 'TORTOISE' on the side of it for a joke and Robbo and the lads had a good laugh at my semi-drugged-up expense.*

"On the bus from the terminal to the plane Robbo was reassuringly telling me not to worry as only one in every 5,000 'planes crash and all the lads were killing themselves laughing. We sat at the back of the 'plane. Alan Moore gave me his headphones and a few CDs I like to take my mind off things and, to be fair, once we were on board the players were all great with me. The flight seemed to go quite quickly and the valium was making me laugh so much I didn't have time to be scared. It was a great feeling when we landed.

"But my Dutch adventure wasn't over, as my luggage went missing once we were back in England. I stayed behind at the airport and looked everywhere without success. When I got home I couldn't believe it was waiting for me on my doorstep after being dropped off by taxi!

"Overall the weekend was probably beneficial to everyone involved. Things have changed over the years. As a player I remember going to

Sweden in the Bruce Rioch era and we were winning games by 12 or 13 goals. Being realistic, when the season started you knew you wouldn't be winning by that amount so it is arguable whether such games were any use. I think they were good for our fitness level but it does depend on the quality of the opposition."

United follow suit

It is also the day Manchester United TV is launched - six months after Boro became the first club to have their own channel. Even though the powers behind MUTV invested heavily to produce their programmes they are soon on their way up to Teesside to see just how Boro TV is made.

Ali: "MUTV and Boro TV are coming at things from entirely different angles. We have grown on ntl's local Channel 8 and developed from two pilot programmes into what we do today. MUTV, on the other hand, have invested lots of money, have a much bigger team and went for the big splash straight away. But, like us, the Sky TV deal means they can't show any matchday action, so to be on six hours a day, five times a week is far too much.

"What you can end up doing is spreading yourself too thin and end up showing too many things that are a bit tedious. If you look at value for money and content Boro TV has grown and grown in terms of what the fan wants to see. They can't take away from us the fact that we were the first football club channel, just like Chris Evans can't take away from us the fact that Bob Moncur's phone-in was the first radio show to be televised. I know MUTV staff get to see copies of our programmes and they have also been across to see how we work. I take it as a compliment that they are interested in what we do."

11 August

Planning ahead

Bernie's About is already establishing itself as one of the most popular features on Boro TV but Ali and Bernie spend the morning thinking of ways to improve it further with much consideration given to who Bernie's future victims will be.

Ali: "We've always planned ahead regarding who Bernie would like to interview. One of the ex-players we were really keen on and approached was Alan Peacock. He played alongside Brian Clough and scored a lot of goals for Boro as well as Leeds United so we thought he'd have some great stories to tell. But the strange thing was, out of all the players we've approached, he is one of the very few to say no. I know of a lot of people who would like him to come on Boro TV. We even did a piece with someone who has worked with Alan and he said he would get him on a show - but, to this day, he remains elusive."

Bernie says: "It's important to have interviews planned but one of the best interviews was actually when we stumbled across a former Boro player almost by accident. We were at the stadium shooting some footage at the time the West Stand corners were being built when we heard that ex-keeper Des McPartland was one of the contractors. We approached a man in a safety hat and it turned out it was Des. He agreed to do an interview and it came out really well. It just shows that sometimes there are things you can't plan. A similar thing happened one night when I was in the Tall Trees nightclub. A bloke came up to me and said he worked with Archie Stephens and from that chance meeting came an interview with the great man himself."

Say cheese

Later the same day the Boro TV team have an appointment at the BT Cellnet Riverside Stadium to capture the events surrounding the pre-season photocall. This is the day when the entire playing and coaching staff from the club come together to have team shots taken on the pitch. Even the youth team are present for snaps - but there are three youngsters in particular who are getting under the feet a little bit.

Ali: "On the day of the photocall Merse's three children were running around. They were also at the training ground quite often around that time so we had seen them before. Although Bernie and I spend a lot of time at Hurworth ourselves we think that most of the time the training ground should be reserved for players only - and not for children.

"It was another indication of how much Bryan Robson and the players tried to accommodate Paul Merson. There we were at the photocall, with club staff working hard to make sure everything was running smoothly, and we all had three little kids under our feet. It was fine making Merse feel comfortable and part of the team, but just imagine the chaos if all the other players had brought their children along too.

"On a more positive note, the photocall gave us the ideal chance to re-acquaint ourselves with all the lads before the start of the season and give the viewers an opportunity to see their favourite team all together."

Bernie: *"If I was the manager there would be none of the players' kids anywhere near the training ground. It's OK having spectators but I feel strongly about the players' children running around. It's a workplace like anywhere else - you wouldn't expect a builder or miner to take their children to work - and there are obvious dangers as well as distractions for the players. And it's not just about the players. These days there's so much surrounding football, for example the many cameras that go along to record training sessions and games, that no-one wants youngsters under their feet."*

15 August

It begins for real - Boro 0 Leeds 0

Everyone is excited as the season gets underway. This is what it's all about and what everyone has missed over the two-month break. Apart from Boro staff, football-mad Bernie and Ali are two of the first people to arrive at the BT Cellnet Riverside Stadium to get ready for their first matchday work since the previous May. The game itself is a bit of a bore and ends goalless but it is a chance for the duo to prepare for the campaign ahead.

Bernie: *"It was the first game back in the Premiership and Leeds is like a derby game so it was important we didn't get beat. A draw was a fair result on the day. The opening game of the season is always like the first day back at school because you have nerves, and it is not like in the pre-season games where it doesn't matter whether you win, lose or draw.*

"For Ali and I it's also where the real work begins, because I think it's fair to say that more people watch Boro TV during the season than in the summer - because naturally that's when there's the most interest in the game.

He jokes: *"The first day of the season is probably the only day Ali is early for anything because there is a lot of work to do like making sure telephone lines, sockets etc. are still working from the previous campaign. When it comes to punctuality, I can say - in the main - that I'm there but when it comes to Ali...well, there's a man that's always late."*

Ali: "It's nearly always sunny on the first day of the season and everybody is looking forward to the return of football. I arrived bright and early at the stadium to bring along the TV and radio gear and spend some time doing any Boro TV interviews and features that needed doing, before going on air for the Century Radio programme at 2pm.

"It was very much like a new year back at college as we had to check our phone lines and sockets in the press box were still working for the season ahead. Then all I had to do was wait for my expert colleague, the Living Legend, to arrive - he's always ten minutes late - and the 'fun' began.

"Of course, there have been times when I've had to do the whole commentary myself. I remember once, during my Radio Cleveland days, when my co-commentator Gordon Cox smacked his head on an iron bar on his way back up to the press box at Hull and I had to step into the breach."

16 August

In the picture

Not only is football back but so are the stresses and strains of being a football commentator. Bernie and Ali are both married with two children and the long working hours and never ending commitments do put a strain on relationships although both men are keen to keep their priorities in the right order.

Former bank manager, **Ali:** "From the age of six when I accompanied my Grandad and Dad on the Holgate End at Ayresome Park, Boro have formed a central part of my life and although my family are more important, inevitably they often take second place.

"When my eldest daughter, Alison, was born, I was at Boro v Notts County instead of the hospital. Alison came into the world at the exact moment Notts County scored their winning goal and, whilst I take no pride from that fact, it reveals what the family tolerate. Boro 1 Family 0.

"When I made the big decision to go full time into the media my wife thought she would see more of me but, as the media has expanded, my family probably see less of me. My only guilty feeling about this job is that I don't give as much time to the family as I should possibly. They keep a picture of me on the fireplace from August to May and then they get to see me in June and July! When my second daughter, Emily, was born my wife, Wendy, and I worked it so we had her outside of the football season."

Bernie: "I sometimes wonder if Ali ever sees his family because he's always either away doing interviews, on Boro TV, on the radio or at a charity event - something he does a lot of. He must only ever see them on a Sunday. There's certainly not as much strain on my family. I see a fair bit of them, probably more than an ordinary 9-5 working man, so I have no room for complaint on that front.

"Of course, football still determines a lot of what's going to happen because most Saturdays are written off for family things but, that being said, my wife Karen is a keen netball player and she is usually out playing on a Saturday herself anyway.

"I have a great bond with my two sons, Dominic and Ryan, and I enjoy spending time with them. Although Karen does all the running about with them I think you'd have to class them as daddy's boys.

"I see them as my little footballers and I believe in trying to get them into good playing habits at a young age. But if they grow up and don't want to play football and do something else instead, that's fine - it's up to them. However, both of them are naturally left footed - just like me - so they are halfway there!"

17 August

I Spy Colin Cooper

Whilst Boro's impressive Rockliffe Park training ground is springing in to life, the project manager Paul Close from Taylor Woodrow gives the Boro TV cameras their monthly walk-around and update as to just how the work is progressing. But this saunter around the 160-acre site is to prove just a little bit more interesting than previous visits as Ali bumps into a player he knew from his first time around at Boro.

Ali: "The building work was coming to an end and the training ground was starting to look mighty impressive so we went for one of our monthly tours.

"We had finished looking around and were walking back to Paul's hut for a cup of tea and a chat when he said he'd seen someone who looked like Colin Cooper. We had a little chuckle and just told him that whoever it was must have snuck past security because everyone on the site - including us - had to wear hard hats. But he told me I needed to put my glasses on and insisted it was Coops. Lo and behold, he was right.

"It can be frustrating as a Boro fan working in the industry when I find out who a new signing is but can't tell anyone. When I go to the pub with my mates the temptation is to tell them all but, of course, there is often too much at stake."

Bernie: "*I remember that Robbo was with Colin showing him around and he looked a bit sheepish when he saw us with our camera because Coops hadn't actually signed yet. It was great to see my old mate Coops back but there is a line of trust between us and the club so, of course, nothing went on Boro TV until a few days later when he officially signed and we got the first interview with him.*"

18 August

Injury for Armstrong

Pre-season 1998 will literally be a painful memory for striker Alun Armstrong as he picked up a horrendous training ground injury. Having just recovered from a bad back injury Armstrong ruptured his Achilles tendon whilst jumping over small hurdles and faced a lengthy spell out of the game. Ali is at Rockliffe Park for the first of many interviews as the Boro TV cameras follow Armstrong's road back to fitness.

Ali: "There are many things that are enjoyable about football reporting - and dealing with Armstrong is one of them. He's a genuinely nice lad with a great family and he's always willing to help out Boro TV. I have a great deal of time for him.

"The day Alun got injured was terrible. Gazza was in tears because he knew of the serious nature of the injury and Alun was rushed to hospital and operated on almost straight away.

"In the following months, we shared Alun's frustrations and hopes as he slowly recovered. Although I wouldn't wish injury on anyone, it made a very good running feature and we spent time with him in the physio room, gym etcetera."

Bernie: "*When I heard Armstrong's Achilles had snapped I couldn't believe it. I felt sorry for the lad and the team because I class him as Boro's top striker. He's a very nice lad - despite being a Geordie - who has not been brought up with a silver spoon in his mouth and appreciates what he's got at this moment in time. He put the hard work in and was dedicated on his road back to fitness and that was great to see as well as capture on the Boro TV cameras.*

"*I see similarities between myself and Alun. Obviously he's a different type of player to the one I was but he's been brought up the hard way like I was and he's grateful for the big chance he's getting at Boro - just like I was.*"

21 August

Coops is back

Four days after the Boro TV crew spots Colin Cooper having a secret look around Rockliffe Park, the experienced defender is unveiled as Boro's latest signing. For Bernie and Ali, it is great to know that someone they both know well is returning to the club but perhaps more so for the Living Legend.

Bernie: *"It was a bit strange because it certainly felt like it was turning into something of a reunion for me. Pally had come back, Stephen Pears had returned as a goalkeeping coach and Mark Proctor as one of the youth team coaches.*

"It was like a flashback but I was happy because I think Coops was a very good signing who has proved you can be just as good second time around.

"I've also always liked him as a lad. Despite what he has done in the game, he's never changed and that's good for everyone who knows him both personally and professionally. He's always willing to do an interview with us wherever possible, as he did almost straight away after signing - at the risk of getting fined!"

Ali: "It was the day Boro TV were guilty of almost earning Coops a fine. We had set-up an interview with him but he had recently picked up a knock and was due in for some physio. We almost made him late and, at one point, physio Bob Ward, Viv Anderson and Gordon McQueen were all shouting at him to get a move on or be fined.

"It was great to see Coops back because I remember when he first came here as an incredibly shy lad with unbelievably long hair. I hope he doesn't mind me saying this but he looked a bit like a waif and a stray.

"I'll always remember a televised game at Ayresome Park when Coops took over in goal from the injured Stephen Pears. He pulled his shorts down to tuck in his goalie shirt and gave stunned viewers a glimpse of his nether regions. We, of course, found the footage and played it as part of the interview."

23 August

On the road again - Aston Villa 3 Boro 1

You've heard the one about how many people can you get in the back of a mini - well, for the Boro TV and Century Radio team

travelling to away games is no joke. Things have improved since the days of travelling miles and miles in the back of Ali's beaten up banger, thanks to a brand spanking new sponsored car, but it can still be a bit of a case of sardines.

Ali: "We do have a much better car to go in now - we call it the rickshaw. It is brilliant because it's a big 4x4 and we can all get in it! But when we first got it we couldn't work out how to change gears and our colleague Rachel Whatley had to drive all the way from Gateshead to Middlesbrough in first!

"It wasn't a great performance against Villa but there were promising signs that the strike partnership of Beck and Ricard was starting to blossom. It was, however, disappointing that Curtis Fleming got injured that day. He is a committed, honest player who tackles hard but unfortunately his career has been littered with injuries so it was a shame to see him hobble off again."

Bernie: *"It was great to get on the road and go to an away game again. Ali is what I would call a good driver - in other words I can go to sleep when he's in control - despite the fact that he usually has his mobile phone stuck to his ear for the entire journey.*

"I met Mark Lawrenson at the Villa game and that reminds me of another match, I think it was against Everton later in the season, when I walked past another former Liverpool great, Jan Molby, in a corridor. I had no idea he knew me but we stopped and chatted and he told me that he knew about my infamous 'bum in Binns' shop-window' (see later text) and that listeners to a Liverpool radio phone-in were encouraging him to do the same thing.

"The game proved to be very one-sided and Villa were deserved winners. Their two wing-backs, Gary Charles and Alan Wright, put in the best performance I've seen in a long time. They had pace, were good crossers of the ball and had everything really."

25 August

Our own Joyce Grenfell

Boro TV's club contact at the training ground is Public Relations Assistant Louise Wanless. Her job involves liaising with the players and setting up interviews as well as organising press conferences.

Ali: "We ca!! Lou our very own Joyce Grenfell - you know, the hockey teacher out of the St Trinian's films - because of her larger than life personality.

"There was a lot of speculation that Paul Merson was leaving and the world's media were at Hurworth awaiting news. Early in the morning Bryan Robson read a prepared statement saying there wasn't much to report because Merse hadn't signed for Villa yet and we had to await further news.

"So we all had to wait around and poor Lou was bearing the brunt of the reporters' frustration as they clamoured for details. Eventually the door of the press room opened but the delight of the press soon turned to despair. Anticipating news on the Merse front, we all waited with baited breath, only for Lou to shout up 'coffee and biccies anyone?'"

26 August

TV evidence

Following an appeal against his sending off in Holland, Paul Merson's red card is revoked. The FA had been sent a Boro TV copy of the incident by the club and this proved to be a significant factor in the charge being quashed.

Ali: "We were there and got the pictures so we were willing to help if we could. It just shows the benefit of recording games and what can be done in hindsight if you have a tape."

Bernie: *"I was delighted because no matter what people think about Paul Merson he's a quality player, and he was Boro's star at the time. It was great that he got off the hook for what should never have been a sending off and even better that Boro TV helped in the quashing of the red card."*

28 August

Double feature

A busy day for Ali and Bernie as two features are on the cards. The cameras are all set to follow Viv Anderson and Gary Pallister to Nature's World in Middlesbrough to see a miniature model of the Cellnet Riverside Stadium and, later on, Colin Cooper returns to the former site of Ayresome Park for a blast from the past.

Ali: "We'd been following the building of the mini stadium, which was put together by a group of students, so it was great to see it unveiled and have two big names there like Viv and Pally, there to help things go along. But I think the only reason we got Pally to go was that Nature's World is near to Bernie's house and he could park his car on the Living Legend's drive!

"Later that afternoon we took Coops back to Ayresome. It turned into a great piece because it was the place he had originally been introduced to professional football and it was brilliant just to watch him sit there on what was a brilliant, warm day.

Bernie: *"The Coops piece was a flashback feature where Ali interviewed him and I on the site of the old Ayresome Park, which is now a housing estate.*

"The two of us sat on a pile of bricks reminiscing. I had been around and seen Ayresome get knocked down brick by brick but Coops had been away and was amazed by how it had changed. He found it hard to imagine Ayresome had ever been there, but it was nice to sit and chat and it made an excellent piece for Boro TV."

29 August

Ham the man - Boro 1 Derby 1

Boro earn their first home point back in the Premiership and Colombian striker Hamilton Ricard claims his first goal of the season. Ali and Bernie had previously seen Ham score a cracker in Holland and realised his potential so it is a joy to see him get off the mark in the top flight.

Bernie: *"We had seen the signs in Holland when Hamilton cheekily chipped the 'keeper from 20 yards out for what was a tremendous goal. He's such a nice lad that we all wished him the best.*

"People were writing Ricard off before he had a proper chance. As a striker myself there were spells when I missed chances, but if you are getting in the right positions the law of averages says you can't keep missing them. But once he had got a goal he looked a more confident player and he continued in a rich vein. He's a lovely big guy who does want to do well so I was delighted for him. When his English gets better I'd love to do a 'Bernie's About' with him."

Ali: "All Ricard looked in need of was confidence at that time as he clearly was getting into all the right positions. In Holland his confidence was perhaps badly knocked because there was a minority of fans being extremely cruel to him with their chants. It had gone from nasty comments to ridicule and that must be one of the worst things possible for a footballer. I felt sorry for him but I always thought he had the character to come through.

"When he put the header in at Derby you could see him starting to become a different player. Even at the training ground he was a different person. Soon after we did a feature on him and his favourite kind of music - salsa. He had excitedly rushed up to us one day with his favourite CD and, to his delight, we even managed to get it played at the ground when he was warming up before the next game."

Making sweet music

Boro TV continue their pursuit of players' hobbies and Bernie interviews Boro defender and spare-time DJ Dean Gordon in a town centre music shop. Some of the best features to appear on the channel have been shot with players partaking in their favourite pastimes and the interview with wing-back Gordon is no exception.

Bernie: "We always ask the people we interview where they want to go and we came to the conclusion that something to do with music would be a good idea for Dean so that he was relaxed. He is good to talk to and things went very well. Coming from London to a place where things work differently and where there are different surroundings can't have been easy but from that day I could see he was settling in quite easily.

"Dean isn't loud or self-centred like some people I've met from the Big Smoke. They are usually way over the top but he is very down-to-earth. In fact he's very likeable for a Cockney! Although I do remember the time my mate Pally got a bit upset because Dean was slagging off his dress sense. But, to be fair, I do think Deano was right - I'm sure Pally still has some of his gear from the 1984-85 season!"

Ali: "We try to speak to players in their comfort zones and Dean is very, very comfortable with the music scene. He used to DJ at clubs when he was in London so we thought it was the ideal thing to do. The problem was that Bernie wanted to stand in the Irish classical music section and Dean wanted to go where the music was a bit more fashionable. Eventually they both agreed to do it in a 'neutral' area of the shop. Dean has got an obvious talent other than kicking a ball around and again another Boro TV feature showed that players do have wide and varied hobbies.

"I remember when we went along to Gianluca Festa's Aikido martial arts class. It was a small room in Middlesbrough and it was the coldest place I've ever been to. I'd never even heard of Aikido, let alone seen people doing it. They were struggling for cash and for members so our piece not only showed Luca's fascinating hobby, but also raised the profile of the Aikido club and helped them get more members and extra cash."

4 Sept

I'll eat my words

Ali goes along to see Bryan Robson for his usual weekly interview on the day 'The Sun' newspaper runs a story saying Paul Merson is set to leave Boro. Robbo has clearly not seen the paper that morning so the intrepid Boro TV reporter is left to tell him - and get his response for the fans. Later that day Ali ends up having to eat his words - literally! - after speaking on his radio phone-in.

Ali: "It was a lovely, warm day and Robbo was in a brilliant mood, having enjoyed a good day off the day before. Sadly, I knew I'd have to spoil it for him by telling him what The Sun had printed. He said 'come on Ali, what's wrong?' and then leant back in his chair. I said I think you ought to read this and gave him a copy of the paper. His response was unprintable! Once he had calmed down he did a chat with us and the Evening Gazette, saying that as far as he was aware Merse was still very happy at the club.

"I went away and did the Century radio phone-in that evening. The subject of most calls was, of course Paul Merson so I said on air that if the story proved to be true and if Merse left by the following Monday I would eat the back page of The Sun I was that sure there was no truth in the story."

Bernie: *"I've done some things in my time but I can't even believe he said he'd do it in the first place. To have to live for a couple of days with the possibility of having to eat The Sun hanging over you must be a dreadful thing.*

"But Ali didn't think he would have to do it because he honestly thought that Merse wasn't going to leave. He was the person who helped bring about the idolisation of him up here by constantly repeating the nickname 'Magic Man' and he believed he was staying. Anyway I would rather do something silly like, I don't know, show my backside in a town centre shop window than eat a copy of The Sun!"

7 Sept

Working lunch

After a weekend of 'will he or won't he?' Paul Merson is on his way south to Aston Villa in a £7 million move. The transfer is met with differing opinions as, on one hand, Boro were losing one of

their best players but, on the other, a 31-year-old player who had hit out at his colleagues is moving on at a £2 million profit just a year after joining the club. And of course Ali will be having a lunch of a very different kind!

Ali: "Merse had gone and I have to say that, after my chat with Robbo, I was a little surprised - and, of course, I'd promised to eat The Sun. I spent the rest of the morning digesting the back page of a national newspaper which was a bit chewy. They even sent along a reporter and photographer to cover the event. If I'd said I wasn't doing it, became awkward and said that I'd only promised to do it as a joke, the paper would probably have taken the opportunity to ridicule me, so I did it. There were also great benefits for Boro TV. We got a picture and mentions in the most widely read newspaper in the country so it was great for publicity. But I still think to this day that it should have been the gaffer who ate the newspaper!

"On a serious note, Merson had always been a focal point of Boro TV with his cardboard cut-out, he had played some brilliant games at the Boro and it is important that everyone - even those who don't like him anymore - remember what he did here."

Bernie: *"I don't think for one minute that when Ali originally said he would eat the paper he did it as a publicity stunt because he didn't think it was going to happen. But once Merse had left, Ali, being a man of his word - or was it because he's mad? - went through with it and that's to his credit. It sums up the kind of guy that he is - very professional but at the same time always game for a laugh and great fun to be around.*

"I have to admit at being a bit surprised that Merse actually left in the end. This was a man who only a few months earlier had gone on national television to say he wanted to manage Boro one day. I could say I wanted to do that but the difference is I would actually mean it. I was also disappointed with some of the comments he made about the Boro lads. I had interviewed Merse and thought he was a nice lad but to come out and talk about a so-called gambling culture within the dressing room changed my views. Of course, some of that sort of thing goes on but it's no different at Boro than any other club or any other business for that matter."

Rude guy - Leicester 0 Boro 1

Boro are on their travels again and are still looking for their first win of the season. With Merson gone, many fans expect confidence to be low but, in fact, it is the other way round as the remaining players are determined to prove a point to the departed star. And who better to come up trumps than the brilliant Gazza. He notches his first goal for the club. Meanwhile, the Boro TV crew are trying their best to do their job despite the presence of a none too helpful PR man.

Ali: "We have that much equipment that I always describe us turning up at away games for Century commentaries as being like Bruce Springsteen arriving for a concert carrying all of his gear, plugging it in and then lighting up the rigs himself before he can even start work.

"But, from the moment we arrived at Leicester, this rude guy firstly wouldn't let us park anywhere near the stadium, then was very suspicious of our cameraman, Graeme.

"We knew and accepted we couldn't film any of the game at all due to rules and regulations - we just wanted to film a feature on what we do at an away game.

"The game itself wasn't brilliant but the winning goal from Gazza was a gem. I thought the biggest plus was the performance of Neil Maddison who was exceptional. I felt sorry for him because a couple of days later he picked up an ankle injury in training and was back out of the team again."

Bernie: *"We couldn't do anything because this bloke was being very arrogant and wouldn't let Graeme into the stadium. We were scuppered and I admit I was getting more and more wound up. Eventually I walked up to the guy and told him he was the most rude and ignorant man I'd ever met in my life. He looked a bit shocked at being confronted but thankfully he backed down and let Graeme in.*

"On the positive side, it was great to get an away win under our belt and Pally had an excellent game against Heskey. Gazza scored a fabulous free-kick and gave the fans a taste of what they are used to seeing from him.

"Pally's storming performance seemed a far cry from 1992 when he was at United and we played against them in the League Cup semi-final. He has had a lot of good games in his time but he was marking me that

day and all I remember was that everytime I got the ball he would run after me and boo and hiss in my ear in an attempt to put me off - of course, it didn't work!"

10 Sept

Junior Reds

As well as his extensive work commitments and tireless efforts for charity, Ali is still connected with the Junior Reds - the second oldest youth organisation connected with a football club in England. It has been around since 1978 and has held meetings everywhere from school classrooms to the BT Cellnet Riverside Stadium. This evening he is again in attendance at one of their meetings.

Ali: "Over the years we have been involved in getting as many youngsters as possible involved in supporting the club. One of the ways we have done this is by having an honorary president - a player or manager - who would come along to meetings and answer questions from the youngsters. We've had some great presidents over the years including Derek Whyte and Craig Hignett, all of whom gave up their free time.

"Being at the meeting that night reminded me of the great times we've had over the years. But most of all I remember when Malcolm Allison, as Boro manager, was involved with the Junior Reds. Big Mal was always one for the outrageous comments and what he had said was that we'd have free training sessions every weekend for youngsters in the community. It seemed a good idea at the time but it quickly went awry. At the first session he arrived and waved his big cigar at the kids whilst talking to them...then disappeared for his Sunday lunch, never to be seen again. Mal was good at starting things - and then leaving them to me!"

13 Sept

What's going on? - Spurs 0 Boro 3

Strange things are happening as a Merson-less Boro romp their way to another away win, this time at White Hart Lane. Meanwhile, following the unpleasant events at Leicester, a kindly steward at Spurs restores Bernie and Ali's faith in human nature. And there is time for a surprise meeting on the way home.

Bernie: "When you look back, that game was without doubt one of the most outstanding and memorable games of the season and it was a pleasure to be able to watch it first hand. One of the advantages of the job that Ali and I do is that we don't miss a single Boro game. Hamilton scored two crackers and was really on form. Although we didn't know it at the time, it also turned out to be Marco Branca's last appearance in a Boro shirt.

"On the way home, we stopped to fill up with petrol and bumped into former Boro star Tony Mowbray, who had been at the game. It was just nice to stop and chat with him. But it was the classic example of how I can never get away from the game - even when I'm at the petrol station!"

Ali: "Our visit to London showed us that not everyone is like the arrogant man at Leicester as a laidback steward let us park next to all the BMWs and Mercs in the players' carpark with the words 'just don't bump into any of the cars, will you?'

"From the minute we parked up we were happy and I had the feeling it was going to be a brilliant day. Hamilton Ricard was on fire in this game as we ripped Spurs apart and got a well earned victory. It was the end of a remarkable week. Just days earlier I had been chewing newspaper because star-man Merse had gone, yet there we were with two great away wins under our belt."

14 Sept

Gilly's about

The interviewee for Bernie on this occasion is former Boro defender Gary Gill who had connections with both Ali and Bernie, having played alongside the living legend and also been a co-commentator with Ali in his days at Radio Cleveland. It is a great chance for Bernie to put some tough questions to his former team-mate but also for Ali to remember the good old days.

Bernie: "I went along to interview Gilly in the clothes shop where he now works and we had a good natter in front of the camera. He is a good story teller and it made a good piece. I know him well as a person and also what he can do on a football field. It is a shame he's not involved full-time in the game anymore, although he still does a wee bit of commentary. When Gilly was on his coaching course he finished top of the class, which is some accolade. He is also a good communicator and a good person. It's sad when you see someone who's played the game and has coaching qualifications drift away.

"It did feel a bit strange interviewing him, as it did with Coops, because these are guys I spent years with in the Boro dressing room and know very well. But whether I know the person I'm interviewing or not, I always enjoy it because every different person is a different challenge and they all have their own tales to tell."

Ali: "I recall one time when Gilly and I travelled to Swansea and sat in the press gantry which was just above throngs of mad Welshmen stood in the equivalent of what was the Holgate End at Ayresome Park. Access back down to the stand was by a rope ladder. From our accents, the Swansea fans knew exactly where we were from so, when Gilly became desperate for a pee, he was too scared to go down to the toilet - so he had to hang on to full-time. Gilly is great because he not only had the ability to play the game but he's also a qualified coach and is very good at commentating. Although he still works in matchday reporting, I think it is a shame his full-time job is now in a different industry altogether."

16 Sept

Wembley memories - Boro 2 Wycombe 0

This Worthington Cup win brings back memories - albeit disappointing ones - of recent Wembley visits and the hope and expectation that another good cup run could be on the cards. Wembley hasn't been a lucky place for Boro over the last few years and the same can be said for Ali and Bernie - although the curse of the twin towers doesn't stop them wanting to return there.

Bernie: *"After the previous Wembley visits it was a case of 'here we go again' and although it wasn't a comprehensive win everyone hoped it would be the start of another good cup run.*

"Although it might have been tempting fate, the victory did remind me of a story from one of our visits to the twin towers two seasons before. We had gone into a restaurant called 'Football Football' in London and I got a good reception as the place was packed full of Boro fans who started singing my name.

"Then, lo and behold, I spotted ex-Boro boss Lennie Lawrence - a man with whom I had had my fair share of well documented run-ins. Of course, I didn't talk to him.

"Thinking back, maybe I should have said 'hello' and I certainly would now. It's all water under the bridge and we all have to move on. There's no point holding grudges - in fact we've since had Lennie on Boro TV as a guest."

Ali: "The victory over Wycombe was a good start to what we hoped would be another lengthy cup run - although three of my previous visits to the famous twin towers had almost ended in disaster.

"At the first League Cup final we almost lost one of the crew when Bernie was driving round and round our hotel carpark testing out our new car. The lad got so nervous he threw himself out of the moving car and took quite a bit of persuasion before he'd get back in. But that wasn't the only near disaster at that final. On the day, we were borrowing equipment from a London-based radio station, but when we got to the ground we found it was the wrong type. Fortunately, a kind-hearted chap from the BBC came to our rescue and lent us some spare gear he had.

"At the FA Cup final against Chelsea that same season the curse of Wembley struck again when we had a run-in with another reporter whilst on air. Wembley officials had accidentally allocated both myself and this other guy the same seat but he insisted it was his, despite being offered a better one by officials. He was getting very irate but there was nothing we could do because we were on air. Thankfully, he eventually stomped off to another seat.

"However our previous predicaments at the national stadium have not dented our desire to return there with Boro and the win against Wycombe only heightened our desire to walk down Wembley Way again - little did we know how things would change later in the season."

18 Sept

Owen McGee

The stars of today and yesteryear are not the only people who are chosen to be interviewed by Boro TV. Those players who have perhaps not quite made the grade or who have gone down other career paths can often also come up trumps when it comes to interesting stories.

Ali: "One day I was in the office and I got an e-mail saying that Owen McGee was at the University of Teesside doing a maths degree and there was a number to contact him on if I wanted to do an interview.

"Owen was part of the Boro team that played at Wembley in the Zenith Data Systems Cup Final in 1990. He was one of the good young players coming through at that stage. But from a very promising start McGee soon left Boro and ended up playing non-league football. He found himself in his twenties and out of professional football.

"The interview was very interesting because it showed how his world had fallen apart around him but how he had rebuilt his life by going back into full-time education and getting a job. It showed the other side of football."

19 Sept

A close shave - Boro 2 Everton 2

Back to the football and Boro throw away a two-goal lead but still maintain an unbeaten home record with what is the third home draw in three games.

Ali: "I blame myself here for what was two points thrown away because I had built up striker Hamilton Ricard a little bit too much with my mathematical equation that if he carried on as he was doing he would score 60 goals by the end of the season. Maybe he knew how much I expected of him and that's why he only notched twice in that game. One thing my prediction certainly did do was get Mr Slaven more than a little bit riled.

"The one thing playing Everton always does, however, is remind me of Nick Barmby and his days at Boro and in particular one time when we'd gone on a horrendously long run of matches without a win.

"I had noticed Barmby had had his hair cut ridiculously short. In an attempt to try and change the luck of the side, I said if Boro won I'd get mine done the same. There was a risk I would look like an escaped prisoner.

"We were playing Nottingham Forest and to my relief they scored first. Then we equalised so it got a bit nervy, but we hung on for a draw and my locks were saved."

Bernie: *"Ali has proved time and time again that he is off his head and he certainly showed it once more when he said that Ricard would get 60 goals over the course of the season. Many people didn't know whether he was joking or maybe just getting carried away because Ham scored two more corkers against Everton. I think he was kidding. He was certainly trying to provoke a response from me.*

"I told him there was no way that by the end of the season he would

even get 20 league goals. As a striker, I know that even if you get off to a glorious start there's always the winter, change of clientele in the side and loss of form to take into account so I knew Ricard would have a bit of a barren spell."

21 Sept

What does Eric do?

Not only are footballers past and present often on the other end of the Boro TV camera. On this occasion it is the Evening Gazette's chief sports writer Eric Paylor. Ali follows the intrepid reporter for the day to find out exactly what he does and just how he manages to fill his column every night.

Bernie: *"Eric is the biggest speculator and teaser in the world. Everything is sensationalism with him. He's like one of the national press, maybe he should work for the News of the World. No, seriously, I'm only saying that to wind him up because I know him well. I appreciate he has to help sell papers with his stories and I know how tough it must be to have to produce a story every night even when things are quiet at the club. He is a good journalist who has been on the Boro trail for years and all the fans know who he is, so it made an interesting piece following him for the day.*

"But it reminded me of just how Eric, with his headlines, can even set his own family against him. There was an occasion when his lad had come out of college with just 50p to his name on a rainy, windy day and had to decide whether to spend it on his bus fare or get a Gazette and walk home. However, on passing a newsagent he read a billboard proclaiming a 'Boro Double Swoop' and his mind was made up - it was to be a paper. Only when he turned to the back page he found Boro were interested in two players on loan from tiny Carshalton Athletic did he discover the truth! I wouldn't like to have been in Eric's shoes when his soaking son came dripping in. Apparently he got a bit of a whack around the head with a soggy paper."

Ali: "We've all seen the caricature of Eric with the big glasses but we thought it would be good to see him at work in a sort of 'a day in the life of' feature.

"We went along with him to the training ground and watched as he rang his report back. It was interesting for us as broadcasting boys as well to see how a scribe works on a daily basis. It was also good to show how Eric is under pressure to produce a back page story every day of the week, whether anything major is happening at the club or not, and just how he does that.

22 Sept

Journey from hell - Wycombe 1 Boro 1

A draw at lowly Wycombe is far from disaster as Boro progress into the third round of the Worthington Cup and are drawn to play Everton. But Wycombe is a long way from Middlesbrough - and the journey seems to take far longer when you stop for a meal with not-so-great service after the game then get caught in the traffic jam from hell on the way home!

Bernie: "We were all happy because Boro were through so decided to stop for a Chinese meal on the way home. We found a restaurant and took to our seats laughing and joking. But the waiters didn't say a word to us throughout and it wasn't exactly what you'd call service with a smile. We weren't rowdy, we just enjoyed ourselves. I have to say the food was very good but it must have been the first time that we've not left a tip, except for 'smile next time'.

"We stayed the night in a hotel and set off back in the morning only to hit the biggest traffic jam in the world. It was massive and I was so bored that half-way home I got out and started collecting conkers for my sons before catching up with the car about five yards up the road!"

26 Sept

They always win 2-0 - Chelsea 2 Boro 0

The Boro TV team hit the road again, this time to Stamford Bridge to play Chelsea, the team who had proved to be the bane of every Boro fan's life in the previous few seasons. Unfortunately, the journey is to once more end in defeat. But it provides joy for one member of the crew, cameraman Graeme Fisher, who takes more than his fair share of stick for being a Chelsea fan.

Ali: "Although I hate to say this, Chelsea were extremely nice to us. They put us in the official car park and treated us very well - I just wish things could have been different out on the pitch.

"However, when we found our press positions, we were isolated at the back of the stand but we had a laugh because the bloke who was handing out sandwiches looked like Richard Attenborough and that

became the standing joke for the day.

"There was a little realisation that day, after winning at Leicester and Spurs, of just how tough the Premiership is. But, to be fair, Chelsea were excellent and we could have no complaints, even though it was annoying when they were singing 'we always win 2-0'."

Bernie: *"The man who had broken our hearts in the FA Cup final, Roberto Di Matteo, came back to haunt us and scored again. To be fair though, it was men against boys and Chelsea were excellent, with Brian Laudrup looking particularly outstanding in what turned out to be one of only a few games for the club. You could tell the fans were thinking 'oh no, not again' and it was particularly annoying when the Chelsea fans started singing 'we always win 2-0'.*

"It was also a bad night for my mate Pally who managed somehow to score an own goal. He was late out of the tunnel that day after receiving some treatment and as soon as he came on he put the ball in his own net. Maybe he should have stayed on the physio's couch."

1 Oct

Boro TV beats Chris Evans

The start of October sees the popular Bob Moncur Football Phone-in - which features Bob and Ali on Century Radio every weekday evening - broadcast on Boro TV for the first time. Not only is this a big step forward for the channel but it also means they have beaten Chris Evans to the honour. A few months after that he claimed his Virgin radio show was the first ever to be televised.

Ali: "We looked at putting the phone-in on Boro TV as another way of taking the channel forward. I thought it would also give us the chance to prove once and for all that Bob wears a wig - hence the name 'the talking toupe'. Bob is great because he pretends to like all the teams in the north-east, but we all know he doesn't. When the cameras are switched off, he's Newcastle daft.

"We beat Chris Evans to put a radio show on TV so that was another first for us. I also managed to get Sunderland's Kevin Phillips on to the show in a rather unique way. He had expressed an interest in coming on so the next time I saw him I wrote out a pretend contract and asked him for his autograph. He didn't know what he'd signed and bingo, he was lined up for the show! Kevin was great on the show. I tried hard to dislike him because he's a Mackem but he's a thoroughly nice lad who you can't help but like."

3 Oct

Let me entertain you - Boro 4 Sheffield Wednesday 0

Boro are back at home and they turn on what ultimately proves to be one of the most entertaining performances of the season with a 4-0 victory over hapless Wednesday. Gazza is on the mark again while the strike partnership of Mikkel Beck and Hamilton Ricard is really starting to come together. But the press have more interesting things to write about than the game.

Ali: "This game proved once again just how much under the spotlight Gazza really is. He stepped up and scored again with a fantastic free-kick yet the headlines the next day were all about whether he wore the right sponsor's boots or not! It was an example of the type of media pressure that was mounting up on Gazza, and that would come to a head a few days later.

"That's why we on Boro TV are keen to take every opportunity to show the real Paul Gascoigne - the one who stops to talk to ballboys after reserve games, gives his shirt away after most matches - to the despair of poor Boro kitman Alex Smith - and does an unbelievable amount of work for charity.

"I remember one funny story about the day Gazza came steaming along to the training ground in his posh Jag and realised he had a flat tyre. I saw him come into reception and, in his usual jokey manner, he was saying 'emergency, emergency'. I asked him what he was going to do and he said he'd get Jimmy 'Five Bellies' to sort it out. Jimmy then came down to look at it and told us what we already knew by saying 'you've got a flat tyre, Paul'. But I'm embarrassed to say none of us knew how to change a flat tyre so Gazza had to call someone from the garage. Some would be surprised that Jimmy didn't know anything about spare tyres!"

Bernie: "It was a very impressive performance from Boro that day but I have to say that Sheffield Wednesday were woeful. But take nothing away from Boro it was a very good result, and an entertaining one at that. The Ricard-Beck partnership was really starting to blossom with big Ham being the main man who was scoring the goals.

"Beck was playing some great football at that time and he was the main source of supply but he always seemed to be the scapegoat when things were going wrong and later in the season - when Brian Deane was signed - I think he was playing on borrowed time. It was just a case of when he would leave, rather than if.

"However, the Sheffield Wednesday game was a particularly good one for him because he got on the scoresheet twice himself. You don't always get the credit for doing the donkey work - but you do for scoring goals. I also think it's important for fans to remember all the goals Mikkel scored in taking us back to the Premiership. He was the top scorer for Boro in the First Division - even above Merson - and that is no mean feat."

4 Oct

Bernie's fear

Once more, Bernie's fear of the skies is put to the test when his footballing friends, Gary Pallister and Curtis Fleming, do their best to persuade him to go on a trip to Dublin. Will he or won't he?

Bernie: *"The lads did their best to persuade me - and I was tempted - but in the end my phobia got the better of me. Anyway, I didn't want to come back with another tortoise! I had thought about driving but that would have been a long, nightmare journey so I thought it was best to say no. Pally and Curtis didn't really have any stories to tell me when they came home, so what they got up to is anyone's guess!"*

5 Oct

Back to School

Thanks to Boro's successful Police projects, where officers of the law are joined by Roary the Lion and travel around local schools educating youngsters with messages on crime prevention, safety and good behaviour, Ali and the team frequently have the chance to return to school. October sees the first birthday of the scheme and Boro TV go along to St Joseph's School in Middlesbrough with some other distinguished guests.

Ali: "We have followed the Police projects on Boro TV ever since the channel started so we were delighted to go along with Robbo, Viv and Gary Pallister to film the birthday celebrations.

"It's great to see the way in which the bond between the Police and the youngsters develops on the projects and, hopefully, it helps breed law-abiding citizens of the future. It is the Police in schools for all the right reasons and that can only be a good thing.

"Everyone really enjoyed the day but the one slight problem is that Roary the Lion was also there. Now the kids love Roary but he does have a habit of upstaging Robbo because he's so popular but I think Robbo's getting used to it now!"

Meanwhile, the first team have two weeks before their next game and take the opportunity to play a friendly match in Ireland against Shelbourne, which they win 2-0. But once again events on the football pitch are overshadowed by the media's insistence in taking part in 'Gazzamania'. It is to be the start of a tough time for the talented midfielder.

Ali: "Stories were coming back from Ireland saying Gazza had had a cigarette at half-time during the game and that on the way back he was found in a railway station in a depressed and distraught state. I just thought that certain members of the national press were enjoying hounding Gazza. Then, a few days later, news broke that he had been admitted to a clinic suffering depression and I just couldn't help thinking that some sections of the media had got what they wanted.

"He had been under the microscope since the famous World Cup incidents in 1990. After playing in that event, there was no doubt he was a world star. The problem is that in this country we put our heroes on a pedestal and then knock them off. Instead of supporting and being proud of a talent like Gazza, the opposite happened and that's a shame because those who know him well will tell you he's an extremely likeable and generous chap."

6 Oct

Stockdale the snooker star!

While the first team lads are away in Ireland it is decided that the Boro TV cameras will follow young defender Robbie Stockdale as he trains with the England under-21 squad. But Ali and Bernie can't make it down to London that day so it is left to the camera crew. They do their best - to botch the feature!

Ali: "We were tied up with other things on Teesside so we sent a camera crew. But first of all they couldn't recognise Stockdale. Then, when they finally got hold of him, they had to decide what was the best way of showing a young footballer training - so they took him to a snooker club and took shots of him potting balls.

"What we wanted was an interview with Stockdale with the rest of the players on the training pitch behind him. So we had to send the cameras back again to do a proper training session. I guess the moral of the story was that if you want something doing, do it yourself."

Slaven heads for Preston

Whilst part of the crew are out with Boro starlet Stockdale, the Living Legend heads in the direction of Preston to catch up with two Boro old boys, Gary Parkinson and Kelham O'Hanlon. According to Slav, it is strange to see the pair at a different club but soon the conversation turns to the good old days.

Bernie: *"I hadn't seen Parky for years although I had kept in touch with what he was up to through the papers and what have you. But as soon as we arrived for the interview it was as if I had only seen him yesterday. We sat at Deepdale (Preston's ground) behind one of the goals and just talked about the good old days. It made a great piece for*

Boro TV. He hasn't changed much. Although he's a defender, he keeps going on about how he's beaten all the Welsh 'keepers because he's scored goals against Neville Southall, Andy Dibble and Tony Norman. Yawn! Yawn!

"Kelham, who is now a coach at Preston, is a funny guy. I interviewed him in his office and he told me about the time he got a letter from a terrorist organisation telling him he had to lose a Boro game on purpose. I don't know if it was his nerves or not but apparently he had an absolute nightmare the following game anyway!"

7 Oct

Mannion's sidekick

Bernie's About takes the ex-striker to the Riverside to interview arguably the greatest player in Boro's history, Wilf Mannion. But the Golden Boy is not alone. He is accompanied by his good friend and sidekick, Albert Lanny, who decides it's he and not the Boro legend who should do most of the talking.

Bernie: "It was touch and go whether we'd get the interview or not because Wilf agreed to do it, cancelled and then decided he wanted to do it again. I had my doubts that when we got to the Riverside he'd want to do it at all. Originally we had arranged to have a chat at Albert's house as that's where Wilf spends a lot of his time. We knew they were good mates so we weren't bothered when he was also in tow for the re-arranged fixture at the stadium.

"Amusingly, the first thing Albert told us when we arrived was that we'd have to talk slowly to Wilf because of his age - I began to wonder if he was his friend or his agent.

"I thought the pair of them were really funny, rather like a double act. And I was extremely honoured to be interviewing Mannion as he's probably the finest player Boro have ever had. But, with all due respect, he is getting a bit old and forgetful. When I asked him who was the best Boro player he had played alongside, he started telling me all about the England side and I had to go over the question again!"

11 Oct

On the spot

Another charity football match is on the cards - but this is a game with a difference. The likes of Boro chairman Steve Gibson and former pro Mark Proctor feature in one of the teams, as does the Living Legend, who has a bit of a score to settle with his friend Ali. The match, which raises money for Teesside Hospice, Middlesbrough Football Club's chosen charity for the year, ends in a 6-2 win for Bernie's side with the wolfman himself grabbing a hat-trick.

Ali: "We went to the Dorman's club in Middlesbrough to record the game. But it certainly was one with a difference. In our Boro TV programme earlier that week Bernie had challenged me to save one of his penalties at half-time. I didn't think Bernie was serious but it certainly showed the power of Boro TV because the crowd were asking for us to do it. Some of them had obviously seen the programme.

"Silly me decided to give so much to charity depending how many Slav scored past me and he promptly scored every one! Of course, I dived the wrong way on purpose because the Living Legend would probably never have talked to me again if I'd saved one."

Bernie: *"There's no way Ali dived the wrong way - he didn't dive at all. In fact, that huge frame of his was totally rooted to the spot. But it was good to see Ali come prepared to be in goal. He had no kit, no gloves and just his normal clothes and big shoes on.*

"We had good fun and the game was for a great cause. The best bit - apart from my hat-trick, of course - was when the linesman kept flagging me off-side. So we swapped places, with him coming on to play and me running the line. Almost immediately, the opposition scored a goal and I raised my flag. I thought it was hilarious until I realised who had scored the goal - a certain Steve Gibson! Fortunately, he took it in good spirits.

"After the game, I realised why millionaires are millionaires when it came to light that Steve had forgotten his towel. I let him borrow mine and told him he could return it to me later. Anyway, he disappeared, leaving me towel-less. When I saw him a few weeks later at another charity do, he told me he'd given my towel away to a wee boy after the game. They'll tell you anything, these millionaires!"

Boro TV exclusive

The close relationship the Boro TV crew have with the club coaching staff often pays off when it comes to breaking stories. And when Boro's star midfielder Paul Gascoigne admits himself to the Priory Clinic with depression, the man who did so much to help the Boro idol, Bryan Robson, opens his heart to Boro TV first.

Ali: "It was the Monday morning after Gazza had been admitted to the clinic and we went to see Robbo. He was very good in telling us what had gone on and let us in on the amusing story that Gazza was organising games of five-a-side and rounders at the clinic.

"At this stage, it really hit home to me that, despite what the papers say, Paul Gascoigne isn't an alcoholic. That's the truth of the matter. Bryan explained that the main problem Gazza was suffering from was depression.

"It also became clear how brilliant Robbo had been in handling the whole situation. He took Gazza to the clinic and made sure he had everything he needed and then stayed in constant touch.

"At the time, he told Gazza that football wasn't the most important thing in his life. He was there for him and he deserves a lot of praise for that."

Bernie: *"Personally, I never thought Gazza was an alcoholic. I've seen him out in pubs and clubs and yes, he enjoyed a drink, but no more so than the next footballer.*

"The weight of public expectation and the press attention puts Gazza under an extreme amount of pressure and it must get him down at times. It must get to the point where he can't trust anyone and he must get quite lonely.

"I felt for him because, even though there's no denying he is a prankster, like I was in my day, he has got a heart of gold. No-one deserves to be followed around and hounded as much as he is by the press.

"A classic example of the rubbish that is written about him was that at that time Gazza had a black eye and some papers were saying he had picked it up on a drunken binge. In fact, he got it through a knock in the friendly game in Ireland.

"One newspaper even challenged its readers to try and spot Gazza in the clinic, offering beer for the best stories. That was just sick. One

minute they were condemning drink and its effects and the next they were giving it away - it was so hypocritical."

13 Oct

Pally op and Townsend roars in

Boro defender Gary Pallister goes into hospital for a knee operation and the latest victim for "Bernie's About" is Boro captain Andy Townsend. Due to his love of and collection of motorbikes, Croft Circuit is the ideal place to do the interview. Boro TV cameraman and biker extraordinaire, Martin Johnson, is the guide for the day. But Bernie has his work cut out trying to keep Andy off the super fast machines.

Bernie: *"Knowing Pally as well as I do, I know he didn't want to come back to Teesside just to see out his career. No way does he ever want to be injured and miss games so I was gutted for him to pick up the injury so early on. But you have to look at his character and I knew with determination Pally would come through it quite quickly.*

"Later that day, I went to interview Andy. The thing I like about him is that he has got a few quid and a few bikes but he is still very likeable and down-to-earth. He is no big time Charlie. Andy felt very comfortable with the environment at Croft and it was a great interview - until he started asking if he could have a go on one of the racing bikes. He was really champing at the bit but we had to say no. Can you imagine what Robbo would have been like if Andy had fallen off the bike and injured himself?"

Ali: "When Bernie went to interview Andy it just reminded me of the story Townsend told me about the 1994 World Cup in America. The team had headed out to Orlando but the hotel was next to a motorway and there was nothing for them to do. The only place they could go to was a hairdressers, so the squad decided they would all have their heads shaved so that when the camera went along the line-up before their next game they would all look tough.

"So, apparently, Roy Keane went first and had his done with all the other lads watching. Once the barber had finished, the rest of them said 'we're not doing it now', so Keane had been well and truly stitched up.

"But it didn't end there. The next day the rest of them said they would have blonde streaks done. So who went first - Andy Townsend. But it wasn't finished by the time the lads had to report back to the hotel so the rest didn't get theirs done - and Andy's was half finished!

"I can just imagine the scene at the next team meeting when Jack Charlton looked up from his cup of tea and spotted Keane and Townsend. The rumour is that he saw Andy and said 'Bloody Hell, we've signed Shirley Temple'."

14 Oct

Robbo and Gazza

The world's media are invited to Rockliffe Park to be told the news that Boro TV already know - that Gazza has returned from the clinic. They are all there to see the midfield genius and are there in their hoards.

Bernie: "More than anything else it was brilliant to see Gazza back at the club, especially as he looked so fit and well. But it was also great to see him sat alongside Robbo. Throughout the whole thing he backed Gazza to the hilt, almost like a father-figure. A good manager should be like that. Bruce Rioch used to say to us that if we had any problems we could go to see him and, as a player, that was appreciated. It also builds up trust. Managers have that role to play.

"It was strange to see so many press there on that day as it was they who drove him into the clinic in the first place. They were the ones hiding up trees and in bushes to get a photo of him no matter what he did."

Ali: "Normally, for a press conference there are two or three camera crews but the place was absolutely packed. It was a strange occasion because here we had someone who had suffered depression, yet again he was part of the media circus.

"He should probably have been allowed to quietly go back to training but the press didn't want that. Just imagine going back to work after being off for a bit of stress and being interviewed by all your bosses at once on your first day back - it is a similar scenario.

"It was like a circus. There were cameras hanging out of the windows and so many people that if they had opened the door some would have fallen out of the room.

"No-one should have to go through what Gazza did that day but, again, what was apparent was how Robbo was by his side again. He sat next to him and gave him moral support and the pair spoke very well.

"I just remember looking around the room and thinking how many of the people there were hypocrites as they had played a big part in putting him in the clinic in the first place."

16 Oct

Deano arrives

Experienced striker Brian Deane arrives at Boro from Benfica in a £3 million deal. His signing is met with scepticism by most fans who are starting to see the strike partnership of Beck and Ricard blossom. But the Living Legend is delighted to see Deane come on board - even if he is a bit dubious about the price.

Bernie: *"As a former striker myself, I was pleased to see Deano arrive. Some people were questioning the £3 million price tag but it is not exactly £10-12 million and those are the prices being banded about for strikers these days.*

"If you look at the likes of Stan Collymore and Kevin Davies, who both went to other clubs for a lot more money and have both arguably underachieved, it starts to look like a bargain for someone who is as experienced as he is."

Ali: "Just like Coops, we'd seen Deane at the training ground a few days earlier so we knew he was going to sign. We call Brian Mr Jinx, you know, the cat off Pixie and Dixie, because his voice is so quiet and similar. We've been trying all we can to get him to say 'I hate those meeses to pieces' during an interview but so far we've had no luck."

Focus on Gibbo

The same day, the Living Legend hits the road to interview Boro chairman Steve Gibson. Despite his wealth and position at the club, Steve is a man who likes to keep a low profile - but he always has time for Boro TV.

Bernie: *"I've known Steve for a long time because he was a director when I was playing at the club. I know him so well that he lets me call him 'Gibbo'.*

"I'll always remember the story that came about after Gary Parkinson, Mark Proctor and I were sold. Apparently, Steve was at a Supporters' Club meeting and was asked why he'd got rid of us and he'd replied 'because they were the Middlesbrough mafia'. I've always wondered what he meant by that but, over the years, I've just forgotten about it. However, this interview gave me chance to find out.

"The interview went well, as expected. Steve is definitely Boro through and through. One thing that proves the fact is that he doesn't own a

Rolex - he wears a cheap plastic Boro watch worth about £2.50. In fact, the chat went so well that I forgot to ask him about my alleged mafia connection. I guess I'll have to just keep racking my brain."

17 Oct

Fleming hell! - Boro 2 Blackburn 1

Boro are back at the Riverside to take on one-time Premiership champions Blackburn. The game is a close affair but Boro come out winners, although there is a very rare occurrence during the game - Bernie's mate, Curtis Fleming, pops up to score the winning goal!

Bernie: *"Curtis had taken a lot of stick, perhaps unfairly, during that game. He had had a bad game but fans have to realise what it is like when you come back from injury. I've been there myself and it's not so easy. Your touch and timing deserts you and on top of that you are back on the big stage where pressure and expectation is much higher than it is on the training ground.*

"Curtis is a tense type of player who always wants to give 100 per cent and do well. Maybe some people don't appreciate that. I know him very well and I was over the moon when he scored that day - it also shut up a lot of the crowd.

"I'll also always remember that match because it's the only time I've ever known fans boil over with anger at my choice of man-of-the-match on the radio. Some people don't accept that my choice is often different from other people's. As an ex-player, I perhaps look for different things but I didn't expect to see what I saw that day.

"The guy who sits in front of the commentary position at the Riverside is usually as quiet as a mouse but when he heard me say I'd given the award to Gordon he started ranting and raving, insisting it had to be Mustoe. Maybe he'd placed a bet on the outcome."

Ali: "I normally do over-the-top excited goal celebrations on the radio but it was Bernie's turn to get particularly excited because his mate got the winning goal.

"Bernie has been accused before of being biased towards the Irish contingent because he used to play for the Republic. He is usually quite fair, I think, but that day he was doing his nut with the fans because they were really getting on Curtis' back.

"When Curtis got the winner, and then celebrated by pretending to smoke a cigar, everyone was then cheering him - no-one more so than Slav."

the red settee

The Big Kick-off - Double act Bernie and Ali launched Boro
TV on the pitch at the BT Cellnet Riverside Stadium.

1. We're Up - A fresh-faced Ali pictured at Ayresome Park just after Bruce Rioch's Boro won promotion to Division One in 1988.

2. Boro Boys - Former Boro player and trainer of almost 50 years Harold Shepherdson was an inspiration for Ali when working with him on Radio Cleveland from 1982-94.

3. Reporters in Need - Ali is pictured with friend and fellow journalist Gordo Cox (left) at a charity event at Ayresome Park.

4. Perfect Perms - For 20 years Ali has helped run the Junior Reds supporters club and he is pictured with ex-Boro kitman Joe Hunt and mate Gordon Cox before their annual 5-a-side competition.

5. Be Prepared - Century Radio's Adam Nolan helps Ali make some last minute checks before a big match commentary at the BT Cellnet Riverside Stadium.

6. A Family Affair - Ali at home with wife Wendy and daughters Alison, 14, and Emily, 9 and Bernie with his wife Karen and sons Dominic, 5, and Ryan, 2.

7. The Big 4-0 - Ali celebrates his 40th birthday with the Living Legend and friends at the BT Cellnet Riverside Stadium.

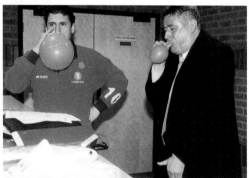

8. Who says Ali is Full Of Hot Air? - Charity balloon blowing is more Gianluca Festa's game than the Boro TV presenter's.

9. Take That - Bernie has a surprise for Juninho-mad Ali on the Boro TV set.

10. Talking Balls -
Bernie's Tactics
Board became a
popular feature with
Boro fans.

12. Behind The
Scenes - Hours of
preparation work
and planning goes
into each and every
Boro TV programme.

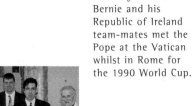

13. Holy Smoke! - Bernie and his Republic of Ireland team-mates met the Pope at the Vatican whilst in Rome for the 1990 World Cup.

14. Old Pally's Act - Bernie has been best mates with Boro star Gary Pallister ever since they played together at Ayresome Park. Pally is godfather to Bernie's eldest son Dominic.

15. Bernie's About - Former Boro star Nick Barmby was just one of the Living Legend's interviewees over the course of the 1998-99 season.

16. It's An Honour - Bernie and the Boro TV cameras went along to the University of Teesside to see Boro chairman Steve Gibson receive his honorary degree.

They were joined by ex-Boro Star Terry Cochrane who tried Steve's mortar board for size!

17. Making Waves - Even in his Port Vale days Bernie enjoyed nothing more than a good sauna - now he's a regular at the Tall Trees Health Club in Yarm.

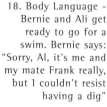

18. Body Language - Bernie and Ali get ready to go for a swim. Bernie says: "Sorry, Al, it's me and my mate Frank really, but I couldn't resist having a dig"

19. Living Legends - The Living Legend meets up with former Boro and Celtic star Bobby Murdoch at the BT Cellnet Riverside Stadium. Bobby would later become a 'victim' of Bernie's About.

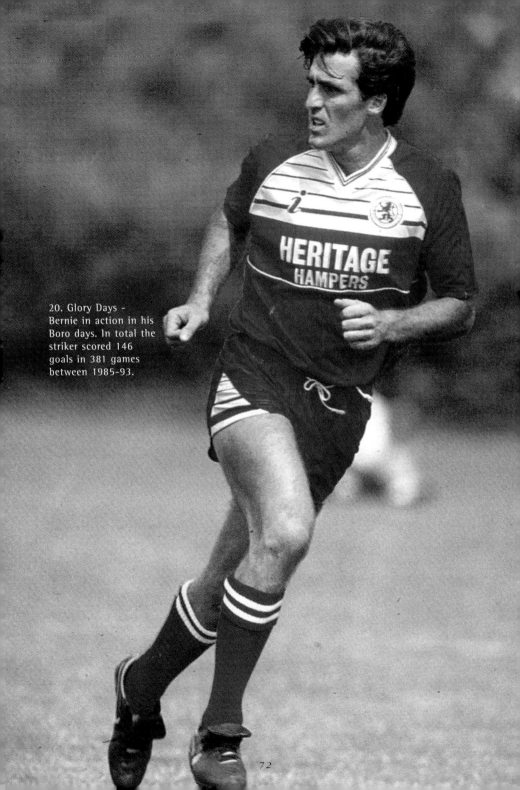

20. Glory Days - Bernie in action in his Boro days. In total the striker scored 146 goals in 381 games between 1985-93.

19 Oct

Queen of Grove Hill

One of the most famous names in the history of Middlesbrough Football Club and world football is Brian Clough. The Middlesbrough-born ex-player and manager enjoyed almost a decade with his home-town club in the 1950s as part as successful career in the game. It was for that reason that the Grove Hill house where he was born and once lived with his family was honoured in the form of a plaque. Boro TV are there to record the historic event and are certainly well looked after.

Ali: "When we turned up at the house, there was this lovely little lady outside polishing the windows and the plaque. We descended on the place en masse and from the off we christened the kind householder the Queen of Grove Hill.

"Once she had finished what she was doing, she invited us into the house, made us a cup of tea and really looked after us. When I asked her what she'd do if Cloughie came back she came out with a great line by saying 'He can come back anytime he wants, I'd polish the front for him as well'.

"When we left the house we suddenly turned into Mulder and Scully for a while after this bloke said they had spotted Cloughie across the road. Of course, he hadn't been there but we kept joking that maybe he'd come to see his house one last time then disappeared off on a number 263 bus at the end of the road."

20 Oct

No-one shouts for Mikkel

After many years working in football Ali, may tell people that nothing surprises him anymore. However, an unusual phone call from none other than Boro striker Mikkel Beck does raise a Brownlee eyebrow - or two!

Ali: "One of the exciting things about working for Boro TV is tracking down people to interview from Boro's great history as well as talking to the modern day figures.

"But one thing's for sure. We usually do all the asking when it comes to interviews. However, Mikkel had other ideas when he phoned up and asked if he could be on Boro TV.

"His reason was more amazing. Because the fans had been on his back quite a bit, he wanted to say how he was trying his best, how he wanted to do well for the club and how important it was for them to get behind him.

"Mikkel is a very clever bloke and he obviously realised what Boro TV is and who it goes out to. It was proof to us that the Boro players know who we are and what we are about and that they trust us in a world where so many people are out to stitch them up."

22 Oct

Bare truth

If the staff at ntl thought they knew everything there was to know about Ali, then this is a day they are about to see something they haven't seen before. Bernie is to get one over on his sparring partner in true footballer style.

Bernie: "When we were in Holland pre-season I had cheekily managed to get a couple of photos of Ali shaving - completely in the buff! He didn't even know I had them and forgot I'd taken them. Then, a couple of weeks later, I remembered, got them developed and started to think how I could use them.

"And what better way than showing them all round the offices at ntl to the delight of thousands of women? Then I gave him the pics and told him I didn't want to embarrass him and that it was our LITTLE secret. You should have seen his face when we next walked through the doors at ntl and all the girls started wolf-whistling and laughing!"

"But I'd never have done something like that to him if he couldn't take it. Ali's game for a laugh and he took it like a true sport, as usual."

24 Oct

It doesn't rain it pours - Wimbledon 2 Boro 2

Back on their travels, Boro pick up a point away at Selhurst Park. However, the long journey south is a nervous one as it pours down with rain all the way. But the game goes ahead and a combination of a great performance from Boro wing-back Dean Gordon and a stunning display from Hamilton Ricard earns Boro another away point.

Bernie: "*Dean Gordon has been a revelation on the left side since his signing from Crystal Palace and he was great against Wimbledon. He showed all his best qualities including his pace, tackling and crossing.*

"*He was getting great balls over and he was a key factor in the good form of Ricard up front who was firing on all cylinders and scored again.*"

26 October

Bye Bye Portakabins, hello luxury

For months the Boro players, coaches, staff and media have had to make do with makeshift mobile Portakabins while the superb new Rockliffe Park training facilities were springing up. But today is the big day as the doors to the luxurious complex at Hurworth are opened to the Boro TV crew for the first time.

Bernie: "*At first, when the Portakabins were there, it used to feel very uncomfortable because the area where we filmed press conferences was right next to the players' changing rooms.*

"*It served a purpose while the work was going on, but moving into the new complex was a real eye-opener. It was magnificent. Many people have said that Rockliffe is one of the best training grounds in Europe and they can't be far off. The players have everything they need from pitches to medical facilities and for those of us on the media side of the fence the facilities are also superb.*"

28 October

Bye Bye Wembley - Boro 2 Everton 3 aet

After three trips to Wembley in a couple of seasons, Boro fans had become used to the odd visit to the twin towers and a home tie against Everton in the Worthington Cup gave the supporters high hopes that they might be heading south again. But the formbook so often goes out of the window in cup ties and that is the case on a cold night at the Riverside.

Bernie: "*We had been spoilt when it came to Wembley cup finals and I think it's fair to say most people thought we would win and be a step nearer the twin towers once more. Everton had some decent players in their side, like Duncan Ferguson, John Collins and Danny Cadamarteri, but they weren't having a good start to the season so to* lose was disappointing, especially as people were harbouring Wembley dreams again.

"The Everton game also showed that you have to be flexible when it comes to working in the media. We were due to have a phone-in after the show but because of the extra-time we had to cancel that and continue commentating - but that's all part of the job."

1 Nov

We were robbed! - Boro 1 Notts Forest 1

Nottingham Forest, the other team promoted automatically from the First Division the previous season, are Boro's opponents at the Riverside. It's an emotional day for Colin Cooper who enjoyed almost five seasons with Forest, sandwiched between his Boro spells. But it is Boro captain Andy Townsend who is once again setting the example - although Sky TV have different ideas.

Ali: "I remember the game as one we most definitely should have won. We were by far the better side and Coops seemed to enjoy himself against his former club who he has a tremendous affection for. Andy Townsend was wonderful and, although Brian Deane scored his first goal for Boro, we gave Townsend man of the match on Century.

"However, Sky gave the award to Paul Gascoigne. Although he had a reasonable game, he played nowhere near as well as Townsend. I just wonder whether they were being a bit manipulative and just gave it to Gazza so they'd get an interview - because it was soon after he had come out of the clinic."

Bernie:: *"It certainly wasn't a classic but what I do remember is that Dean Gordon was well and truly marked out of the game by Steve Stone. He was having a great season but it was becoming apparent that other teams had sussed out how to play against him.*

"It was also a big day for my old mate Coops, who was playing against his old club. It's nice to see your friends again and even better if you are able to beat them on your return - unfortunately, he had to settle for a draw that day."

2 Nov

Meetings, meetings, meetings

Boro TV is growing all the time and audience figures are swelling, but it is felt that to keep moving forward progress meetings should be held every Monday to discuss programme ideas as well as long term plans. These are soon to become an integral part of the working week but one or two of the little get togethers are a bit strange to say the least.

Bernie:: *"The meetings have been very effective and have led to an all round improvement in the standards of Boro TV in my opinion. In the* *past, because people's roles had become mixed a little bit, Boro TV was in danger of becoming just one or two people's ideas and that could have had a negative effect.*

"The first six months of Boro TV consisted of a lot of things being done off the cuff but now there is a formula and the meetings mean we can keep moving forward all the time.

But on occasions they are certainly very entertaining to say the least and I really enjoy them when we get bacon sandwiches!"

Ali: "Peter Wilcock, who is ntl's Head of Sales and Marketing, decided that the best thing for us to do was have a meeting so that all members of the Boro TV team and representatives from the club and so on can have their say.

"They have gone really well and I think improved the standard of the programmes. The meetings can vary from quite calm 10 minute chats to quite heated debates. But they've also had their, shall we say, eccentric moments.

"I remember being staggered when Peter suggested we watched an episode of The Hair Bear Bunch at the next meeting. And, lo and behold, the following Monday we all sat and watched it on video. To this day I'm not sure why, but Bernie thought it was hilarious!"

Anyone for tennis

The same day the Boro TV team set off for the latest "Bernie's About" and, in looking for a unique setting for the feature, they arrange for Bernie to play tennis against Boro defender Gianluca Festa - a former Sardinian youth champion. It's supposed to be just a bit of fun but thanks to Ali, Mr Festa thinks he's in for a bit of competition.

Ali: "Bernie had claimed that he could play tennis and Festa kindly agreed to come along. But that's where the whole thing went wrong - because Bernie had never actually played the game in his life before.

"Anyway, Luca arrived about an hour early and was practising his serves anticipating Bernie to be something special. It didn't help that I falsely told Luca that Bernie was the Scottish tennis champion - but inside I knew Bernie was about to be trounced.

"Then Bernie turns up in his old raggy tracksuit and as soon as the game started I was proved right as the first serve almost took Slav's head off. In fact we had to fix it so that Bernie could return one of Luca's shots and get a point! But it was a great feature for Boro TV. It was away from the 'this is a footballer, this is the training ground' type of interview which can have everyone dozing off."

Bernie:: *"It was totally rigged. I've always been a big admirer of Festa, so when Ali asked me if I wanted to play him I said no problem. I told Ali that I wasn't very good but when I turned up there was Luca stretching and practising his serve in his pristine white shirt, shorts and socks. There was me looking a real raggy-arse and he was looking like an immaculate Pete Sampras.*

"He was taking it seriously and I was trying to tell him that Ali had set me up but he must not have understood because he battered me out on the court. We had to use the tricks of the TV trade just to make it look like I wasn't totally useless!"

7 Nov

"You can't park here" - Southampton 3 Boro 3

The Boro TV team are on their travels again - this time to Southampton on the longest away trip of the season. The mood is good following a promising run of results, but that is soon to change. After a five hour plus journey south, they meet a man who Ali later calls "the world's most obnoxious car park attendant" and are then forced to sit in a cramped goldfish bowl-like press box to watch the game.

Bernie:: *"Normally what happens when you arrive at a ground is that you either have an official car park pass or you have to try and blag your way into a car park. It's important to be quite near the stadium due to the amount of equipment we take.*

"When we arrived at The Dell, we made our way to a nearby school carpark, and Ali came out with his usual line 'We're from Boro TV and Century Radio, coming to you from the heart of the north-east'.

"But the attendant just said point blank 'you can't park here for nothing'. So we asked him how much it was and he replied 'I'm not telling you'. He even had the cheek to say he wasn't letting us on the carpark because of OUR attitude! He was obnoxious and arrogant and I ended up telling him where to get to. We finally found somewhere to park and went up to the press box, which is behind glass, and loses something of the atmosphere in my opinion.

"There was a lot of talk about Gazza possibly being in the England squad and he was being watched by Glenn Hoddle. He responded by having a very good game and looked great on the ball but I would have

to say he didn't look international class even though the hypocrites amongst the national press raved about him the next day."

Ali: "The press box is quite small so all the media have to squeeze in and we ended up tucked in behind the door. Then, five minutes into our commentary, this portly chap came in to bring some food for us, but instead of trying to creep in he came in shouting 'sandwiches, sandwiches' as we were broadcasting live.

"Strangely he didn't seem to realise we were working and gave the sarnies to me. I passed them on to Bernie but as he tried to hold the food and watch the game at the same time he fell off his stool dropping the sandwiches everywhere.

"Everyone was looking at us and by this time Bernie had his foot in the sandwich tray under the desk. But Slav being Slav he just removed his foot, turned the sandwiches over so his footprint couldn't be seen, and passed the tray along to the journalist next to him."

10 Nov

Bernie tracks down Alcock

Following a none-too impressive performance from controversial referee Paul Alcock in Boro's game at Southampton, what is arguably Boro TV's most popular and entertaining feature so far is made. Bernie, the intrepid Boro TV presenter, sets out to track down Alcock (well, an Alcock look-a-like from Middlesbrough) - and finds him in the most unusual of places.

Bernie:: *"I decided I would go and look for Mr Alcock after his disappointing performance at The Dell. We had originally come up with the idea of following him to the massage parlour but decided it was a little too seedy for Boro TV!*

"So we went into the heart of Middlesbrough and knocked on the door of his house, but despite plenty of shouting through the letter box he didn't answer. I knew he was in there so I waited in the car - then all of a sudden 'Mr Alcock' made a run for it.

"The next thing the viewers saw was the disgraced ref aptly making an appearance in the opticians before making his way to the local school to referee a kids' football match. I then rushed onto the pitch and in a scene straight out of a Carry On film I push him on his backside.

"It was one of the funniest things we've ever done on Boro TV and the guy who pretended to be Alcock (he works at ntl) played the part

brilliantly. In fact I believe he still gets called 'Alcock' when he walks down the street and every time I see him I still call him ref!"

14 Nov

Bernie comes of age - Charlton 1 Boro 1

It's another away game for the crew but this one has a special edge to it as it is the day after living legend Bernie Slaven's birthday. Another away point helps him celebrate in style but he is still upset that Ali has a state-of-the-art pair of headphones to wear while commentating - yet he has a pair that probably date back to around the First World War. He wants a new pair and it's a point he makes in spectacular style.

Ali: "Bernie was enjoying his birthday in typical away match style by handing round the chocolate and drinks and getting rubbish all over the Century Radio car along with the rest of the crew on the journey south. But once we were at Charlton he was soon in a grumble and the main reason was that I had a state-of-the-art pair of headphones. He had been jealous all season but he thought that because it was his birthday Century might have got him a new pair as well.

"During the Charlton game we had a few technical problems that made us sound like we were recording from a tin can in the middle of space and it got worse at the end when Bernie finally flipped. He said something about Century being skinflints and then took his headset off and threw it on the floor in sheer disgust. Luckily I managed to persuade him to pick it back up and we continued with the commentary."

Bernie:: *"Ali had bought me a Jock Stein book for my birthday and in it he had sarcastically written 'A book about a legend for the living legend' and Rachel from Century bought me a George Michael CD, which of course I played all the way to Charlton to the absolute delight of the rest of the crew. But the best present of all was also from Ali. He got me a pair of inflatable boobs that you blow up and rest your head in between when you're having a bath. Everybody should have a pair, in fact Ali has got his own!*

"However my new headphones certainly didn't arrive in the post and I had to put up with Ali showing off his state-of-the-art pair. But I complained a few times to the listeners during the Charlton game and eventually my bosses gave in and I got some as well."

Bright young thing

Boro youth coaches Stephen Pears and Mark Proctor speak to Ali about the possibility of taking the Boro TV cameras along for a chat with young Australian midfielder Luke Wilkshire. Like Aussie 'keeper Mark Schwarzer before him, the dedicated 16-year-old has made the brave step of travelling halfway around the world to pursue his dream of becoming a professional footballer.

Ali: "Luke is a great kid with a great deal of potential and even more maturity for someone who is so young. I just remember thinking about my daughter as I was talking to Luke. She is a similar age to him and I wonder how I'd cope if she came to me and said she wanted to go off to Australia on her own to forge a new career. It's the same sort of thing.

"But Luke is coping remarkably well and showing a lot of inner-strength. In Boro's Academy they teach you how to handle the media, how to present yourself and so on, so he came across very well too.

"He talked about how he was a little bit homesick when he first arrived and how he has made friends and adapted to life over here. I have a lot of respect for him and I hope he goes on to be a great player.

"He has certainly made a big commitment to try and do that and his story is very similar to that of Craig Johnston who also came to Boro from Australia and went on to have a very successful career in the game."

Super Shilts

On the same day, "Bernie's About" takes the living legend to The Emerson Arms pub near the Hurworth training ground to interview legendary 'keeper turned coach Peter Shilton. Shilts, who learnt his trade as understudy to Gordon Banks, is the man in charge of looking after the likes of Mark Schwarzer, Marlon Beresford and the younger 'keepers at the club.

Bernie:*:* *"I met Shilts at The Emerson Arms and straight away I got the impression he was a bit suspicious about what I was going to ask him. I asked him about the infamous 'Hand of God' goal and then I had a bit of fun with him about the second goal Argentina scored that day. I told him that as a Scottish-born lad who played for Ireland I was jumping around on the settee when the Argies scored and he just laughed.*

"He told me a great tale about when he was younger and because he'd always wanted to be a 'keeper, what he would do to try and make himself taller. It turns out that when he was a kid he used to hang from the bannisters to try and make his arms longer. Can you imagine visiting the Shilton household and having to say to Mrs Shilts 'Good morning, is that your Peter hanging from the bannister again?

"Shilts is a good guy who was great to talk to and obviously he was a quality goalkeeper. It's great for Boro that we have someone like him looking after our 'keepers of the future."

20 Nov

Rolando not Ronaldo

Three days later and it's another former 'keeper for Bernie's About as the cameras turn to Rolando Ugolini. The Italian-born former Boro player turned out at Ayresome Park from 1948-57. As well as being a tremendous shot stopper, he was known as a real joker on the training ground and Bernie went along to hear his tales.

Bernie: *"Rolando played for my other favourite team, Celtic, as well as being the first Italian to star for Boro so I was really keen to speak to him and we arranged to get together in a Middlesbrough hotel.*

"He was a really nice guy but it was apparent from the off that he had been a bit of a prankster during his playing days - rather like myself and my former team-mate Trevor Putney - and I liked that about him. The interview also showed that over the years footballers' humour hasn't changed.

"One of the best stories he told me was about the time coach George Camsell pulled up at training in a brand new, black car. Whilst all the lads were out on a run Ugolini snuck off, got the groundsman's white paint and painted the car entirely in white. Apparently after training it took George quite a while to find his car - but when he did he went absolutely berserk.

"He also told me about one time when he was staying in a hotel and he went behind reception with a stocking on his head and told the receptionist to put her hands up. To his dismay she fainted on him."

21 Nov

Strachan goes ballistic - Boro 2 Coventry 0

A convincing home win continues Boro's good run of form but it is Coventry manager Gordon Strachan's post-match press conference which makes the headlines. The Scot's manner is unusual to say the least and Bernie and Ali are present to witness the events.

Ali: "Gordon Strachan's post-match interview was so bizarre we even included it on an out-takes video at the end of the season. It was hilarious. He came into the press room and the way he acted was almost as if he was someone who had been in a pub all afternoon or was itching for a fight because whatever anyone asked him he bit back aggressively.

"At one point he was asked where the game was won, meaning which area of the park, and he answered 'on that green thing out there'. That set the tone for the entire interview and we didn't really get much sense out of him.

"However, Chris Kershaw from Boro's Public Relations Department, who had brought Strachan upstairs for his interview, later told me he had been a smashing bloke on the way up. It all seems a bit of Jekyll and Hyde to me."

Bernie:: *"Strachan was very sarcastic, but I liked him that day to be honest. At the end of the day the press will write what they want anyway so it didn't really matter that his answers were abrupt one-liners.*

"It was a terrible performance by Coventry and he was no doubt extremely annoyed by it so that would have had a bearing on what he said. We later put the whole press conference on a Boro TV video called 'Oddballs and Out-takes' to give Boro fans a good laugh."

27 Nov

The chairman is honoured

Without Middlesbrough Football Club essentially there would be no Boro TV and, arguably, without Steve Gibson there would be no football club - at least not one that is as high profile and successful as it is today. So it was apt that the Boro TV cameras went along to the University of Teesside to film Steve being presented with an honorary degree.

Ali: "Steve was being honoured not only for the work he has done for Middlesbrough Football Club but also his business Bulkhaul and what he has done for the town as a whole.

"As well as giving people a stable team to support, he has also been responsible for giving many a job and a livelihood, which is perhaps even more important than football.

"But it has to be said that most people on Teesside see him as Mr Football first and foremost. We were honoured to be there on such a special occasion to film events and have a chat with Steve."

Bernie:: "*We were sat near the stage and Steve's family were sat just in front of us. Alun Armstrong was representing the club and he was sat next to me. That soon became a recipe for disaster when one particular guy with a rude sounding surname came on to do a speech.*

"*Both Alun and I burst in to fits of laughter and this continued right through the next bloke's speech, because he was just talking a load of old jargon and long words. As a footballer and ex-player of course the pair of us couldn't understand a word! We were not purposely trying to be rude - we just got the giggles it was so hysterical.*

"*Steve fully deserved the honour for everything he has done for the football club and the people around here and it was a pleasure to be there. When he was a director, I was a player and although I never really mingled with him, I knew what he was trying to achieve and most of that can be seen today.*

"*The majority of chairman are in the game because of their love of money but he's in it because of his love of Middlesbrough Football Club. He's a Boro fan and I take my hat off to that.*"

29 Nov

Bernie's Valium trip and Mikkel's Restaurant - Arsenal 1 Boro 1

Having travelled to the likes of Chelsea and Southampton earlier in the season, you would have thought the journey south to Arsenal was an easy one to make. But for Bernie it was a little more difficult than the others as he battled with his nerves. But why nerves, surely Arsenal aren't that good? The reason was that early the following day the Boro TV crew would be flying (yes, flying) out to Madrid to interview the one and only Juninho - and hopefully Bernie would be with them!

Ali: "The away day at Arsenal has since become known as Bernie's Valium trip. On the day of the Arsenal game I checked that Bernie still wanted to come to Madrid, which he did, and made sure he had his passport before setting off south.

"On the way to Highbury he popped one Valium and just before the game he dropped another. But the problem with them is that they do make you very relaxed and it didn't go un-noticed by the Arsenal press officer who I overheard say 'have you seen that Bernie Slaven? He looks half drunk lately!'

"As I announced the teams I half expected Bernie to start snoring but he managed to hold out. Then, as we finished the commentary, came the bombshell. Bernie announced that his fear had got the better of him and that he wouldn't be coming to Madrid.

"We always suspected he might change his mind and I didn't want to push him so we waved bye bye to Bernie and went our separate ways. We were gutted he couldn't make it but still excited at the prospect of meeting up with the little man again."

Bernie:: *"I was spaced out that day because I was on Valium in the hope that I'd make it to see Juninho. Before the game I'd met up with Brian Little, who was a coach when I was at Boro, and I was telling him how much I was looking forward to Spain. But deep in my mind I knew I wouldn't go and after the show I plucked up the courage to tell Ali. I could tell he was a bit disappointed but so was I.*

"I have said a lot of things about Juninho that some people don't agree with, but nothing I wouldn't say to his face. I like the lad a lot, I just don't agree with the way he left Boro and I would have gone and asked him some tough questions, so from that point-of-view it was gutting to miss out.

"We got a draw that day but it could easily have been a win. It was great to see big Deane get on the scoresheet again and he probably should have had another couple that day."

Ali: "That night we were invited along to Mikkel Beck's new Danish restaurant in London. We had a great evening and the food and setting was excellent. It was also good thinking by Mikkel to use Boro TV to help get his new business off the ground."

JUNINHO-O-O

It's an early rise for the crew as the day has come to jet off to Spain for the exclusive interview with Boro legend Juninho. The journey to magnificent Madrid is a bit of a challenge to say the least but it all becomes worthwhile when they meet up with the little man and his kind family. An enjoyable weekend is had by all and another brilliant Boro TV interview is in the bag - but not without life's little test along the way.

Ali: "We woke up to our alarms at 5am and hardly had the chance to realise it was the day to go to Madrid. But we had no time to dwell as we had to check in by 5.50pm.

"It was a shame the fear of flying had cut the wings of the living legend as the interview was to be a balance between the Slav putting across his view of Juno as a rat who left the sinking ship and I was to concentrate upon how he feels about life in Madrid and his future.

"And with him missing it left the cameraman and I to carry the equivalent of the equipment Napoleon took to Moscow between the two of us. Our former colleague Simon Hanning, who lives in London, was invited along in Bernie's place.

"The courtesy bus arrived, only it was not really a courtesy bus, and we didn't have a penny between us - our cash was all in pesetas. Thankfully my Visa card was accepted at the airport hotel desk and we got on.

"By the time we'd taken the bus - and believe it or not a train! - to Terminal Four it was 6pm and the check-in desk was closed. I began to wonder whether the little genius was worth a heart attack and also what our bosses would say if we failed to make the flight.

"The check-in clerk gave us a look of thunder as she looked at our tickets and then asked us to take all our equipment as hand luggage. Things were getting really out of hand especially when she realised that Slaven's ticket was accompanied by Hanning's · passport. We were forced to leave Simon with airport security while they made further checks and Graeme and I raced to the departure gate to be followed by the security men.

"Finally we were marched onto the plane and our equipment was wheeled in another direction with a promise that it would reach Madrid, probably the same time as Spring but quite frankly I was too knackered to care. Then the pilot announced we had missed our flight slot and a hundred pairs of eyes stared at us accusingly."

Madrid

Ali: "The capital of Spain was cold but the arrival at the hotel was warm. In an attempt to show the strength of Spanish manhood, our driver angrily shrugged off any attempts at assistance in picking up our camera case which he judged to be light. A slow swing in the air and the force of gravity put out the driver's rear light with a horrible smash and the gutted cabbie had a face like thunder.

"Our hotel was modern and pleasant, unlike the mood of the porter who carried our Boro TV gear to our room only to find that I have lost the pesetas - no tip! In an attempt to restore sanity I ran a bath. It was 3pm and time to relax with the Juno interview 24 hours away. So I rang interpreter Zelia Knight to check everything is OK. But I was shocked to hear the words 'Alastair, Juninho cannot do the interview tomorrow, it has to be 4pm today. See you in an hour.' So it was action stations.

"I remember our porter bravely carried the gear back to the door, again for no tip, and reception handed me a note. Simon had called and I couldn't believe it. For some reason he was in Brussels!

"The taxi sped towards Juninho's house where we were welcomed by the family. I had wanted to dislike Juninho for leaving the Boro and in the absence of Slav, take a tough approach. But he was the same likeable young man I had met at the Riverside and I couldn't bring myself to do it.

"I thought the interview would just go with the flow until I heard 'Alastair..Juninho would like to do the interview in Portuguese'. It was typical of the way things were going. Thankfully a little persuasion worked and Juninho did the interview in English saying that he holds out some hope that he may return..one day.

"For the record, my view of Juninho is that he is the best player I have seen in a Boro top and, for all the remarks that he left the sinking ship, he certainly didn't put the hole in it. He nearly, almost single-handedly, saved Boro from relegation. Surely the scene of a distraught Juninho at Leeds after Boro were relegated should haunt doubters of his commitment.

"After what turned out to be a great interview we enjoyed a family meal interrupted by occasional snores from an exhausted cameraman. Juninho revealed after the interview an in depth knowledge of the Premier League and the abiding memory is of a player who is unhappy with his club and who will probably move on in the short term.

"After tea we returned to the hotel and en-route I tried to join in the Bob Moncur Football Phone-In, from Spain, on a mobile, on the back seat of a taxi - a recipe for disaster in anyone's book!

"The following day, after breakfast, Juninho's father kindly picked us up to take us to the training ground but, unfortunately, got lost on the way. When we arrived the press coverage of training was stopped as we tried to explain to the other media there that us having the cameras there didn't mean Juninho was about to re-join Boro. We made the Sports section of Marca - one of Spain's biggest papers - because of that. Great publicity for Boro TV! Thankfully our return the next day was less eventful than the outward journey and we all get back tired but in one piece."

6 Dec

Bob Moncur at the Riverside - surely not! Boro 2 Newcastle 2

Another point is earned but it really should have been three as Boro impress against their local rivals. Twice the lead is thrown away but perhaps a more impressive sight is the one and only Bob Moncur, sat in the press box at the BT Cellnet Riverside Stadium. As Ali says, it is something he never thought he would ever see. Bernie, meanwhile, has his own views on why the derby wasn't exactly a classic.

Ali: "It was amazing that my radio colleague Bob was let in at all, because the talking toupee had been wittering on all week about how Newcastle were going to beat the Boro. So I'd primed a few of the stewards not to let him in but somehow he managed to get himself into the press box - maybe he wore a disguise!

"Bob tries to claim that he supports all the teams in the north-east but that's a load of rubbish because he's a Newcastle fan first, Sunderland second, Hartlepool next, then Darlington with Boro coming in some way behind.

"Despite a great atmosphere on the day the game itself was disappointing because we took the lead twice only to throw it away both times. You always want to get one over on your local rivals, but it wasn't to be."

Bernie: *"I don't think derbies possess the same passion as when I played. I'm not talking about a change in attitudes over 30 or 40 years - more like the eight or nine since I was a player. In my day they were all local lads - Stuart Ripley, Colin Cooper, Gary Pallister, Tony Mowbray and an adopted Teessider called Bernie Slaven - but these days that's not the case.*

"You only had to look at the Newcastle team that day to see there were more foreigners than anyone else. I don't think they are aware of what derbies are all about and, although there is still passion amongst the fans, for the players it's just another game.

"I remember Jamie Pollock saying 'I hate the Geordies' in an interview after his first derby. In hindsight he probably wishes he didn't say that but it is an example of how the occasion had given him an adrenaline-rush and how much it meant to him."

7 Dec

What a picture

With Christmas looming the Boro TV boys get their heads together to discuss the making of a festive video. After several meetings they decide to make a tape called Oddballs and Out-takes which will feature one or two of the more unusual moments and mistakes from the first series. But it is the cover that will accompany the video that raises the most hilarity.

Ali: "We'd had a few thoughts about what we could do, like doing a best of Bernie's About, but we decided to look through the archives and find funny moments such as when Bernie dropped the microphone or where I had had a slip of the tongue.

"It was a bit like 'It'll be alright on the night' and we really enjoyed putting it together - except we weren't told that the cover would make Bernie and I look like a couple of Spitting Image puppets. When we saw it for the first time we couldn't believe it. There was me looking like the elephant man and Bernie looking like that famous Norwegian painting 'The Scream'. But, after harbouring thoughts of suing somebody, we decided it was appropriate because it showed that it was a funny video - although I have to say my mum did refuse to buy it because of 'the ridiculous picture on the front cover'."

Bernie: *"They took a normal picture and then used technology to stretch it. They stretched Ali's a wee bit more than mine but then again there's more of him to stretch. It was a bit daft but obviously it went with the title of the video and I think it worked well. All that said I also thought Ali looked better on the cover than he does in real life!"*

9 Dec

Whitby Ham

In-form Boro star Hamilton Ricard has got his scoring on track by this stage of the season but his next challenge is to be on the railway as Boro TV take him aboard a steam train at Whitby for their latest feature. It is a task the Colombian relishes as he gets to grips with a large locomotive - the only problem is the language barrier.

Ali: "The funny thing was that Hamilton just didn't have a clue what was going on. At the time his English still wasn't up to much and as we picked him up at the stadium and bundled him in the car he must have thought we were kidnapping him!

"Trying to explain to a Colombian that you are taking him on a steam train and then for fish and chips isn't the easiest job in the world but he did understand a reference to Whitby being Dracula's home as he had heard of the fanged one before.

"Hamilton was dressed for a formal day out in a white shirt and although he was impressed when he got his first glimpse of the steam engine, he was less so when he ended up covered in soot!

"But he had a great time on board the train. He soon worked out how to blow the whistle - and proceeded to do that all the time - and before long he had worked out how to move the thing backwards and forwards. The only problem was that he was so enthusiastic that he hit the lever and we shot off towards the station far too fast for our cameras to film. Then Hammo did the same in reverse, whilst hooting the horn and cackling out loud. Eventually he did slow down and we got a great feature out of what was a great day."

Bernie: *"Interviews like that are great for the people who watch Boro TV. It's great for them to be able to tune in and see players from different countries, with different mannerisms and cultures.*

"It would be easy to focus on the likes of Robbo and Gazza all the time because they are the most famous names, but it is Boro TV, so we feel it is important to feature everyone connected with the club, and the Ricard interview was a good example of that."

10 Dec

On the Net and Gilly's About

The tables are turned when Bernie becomes interviewee as former team-mate Gary Gill springs a surprise by bursting into his house with a camera crew and interviewing him for Boro TV. Later the cameras are at the Riverside to record the launch of Boro's official Website. The club's decision to go on-line offers the fans a service to use for all the latest news and views, but it also has other advantages.

Ali: "Gilly snuck into Bernie's house like a kind of 'This is your Life' type of thing and caught Bernie sat eating a plate of chips. It almost went pear-shaped when Bernie's dog set off barking after Gilly but when things calmed down it was Bernie's turn to be asked the questions.

"Once Bernie had got over the surprise we had a great laugh and Gilly did an excellent job though we almost missed our next job because Bernie waffled on that much. He virtually talked us through every one of his goals!

"We raced to the stadium and got there in the nick of time for the launch of the new Internet site which we were keen to cover because it is something that is very advantageous for all involved.

"From our point of view it's great on two fronts. Boro fans who live outside the area and can't listen to our Century commentaries can get the audio on the website and there's also a section on Boro TV which contains interviews and a whole lot more."

Bernie: "The Gilly thing was a complete surprise - I was done up like a kipper! Looking back it did seem a bit strange that day because on the way back from the studio Ali suggested we go to my house to get something to eat and he'd never done that before.

"Anyway we were both sat there eating fish and chips when Gilly burst in and nearly gave me a heart attack. But when I regained my composure the tables were turned and Gilly got stuck into me with some searching questions.

"I talked for a while about my career, how I got into football and things like that. Gilly did great but I didn't lose my job because 'Gilly's About' doesn't have quite the same ring to it - does it?"

12 Dec

What a cheek! - Boro 1 West Ham 0

Another great home win has the fans in raptures but it is Bernie who amazingly has the bare cheek to promise to show off his bum in Binns window if Boro can win their next game - away against giants Manchester United. It all points to an extra incentive for the Boro lads but surely Boro can't win at Old Trafford, can they?

Bernie: "Forgive the pun but it really was tongue-in-cheek. The saying 'I'll show my bum in Binns window' has been popular in the area for a long time and it sort of means 'there's no chance of that happening'.

"I didn't think we would beat Manchester United at Old Trafford. They are a quality side and I felt that a draw would be an excellent result so I was quietly confident that I wouldn't have to take my trousers off."

Ali: "It was the classic example of before you ever say anything, make sure you engage your brain first. But what it did prove is that sometimes the simplest of phrases can have the biggest of consequences.

"Bernie had been going on a little bit about how good Man Utd were and how it would be a miracle if we beat them and I asked him what he would do if we won. His answer 'I'd show my bum in Binns window' has now become infamous on Teesside and beyond!

"I soon got the idea that it was all being taken seriously because as we left the ground there was a group of fans and a couple of them said 'Bernie, we're looking forward to seeing your bum'. Then on the Bob Moncur phone-in on the Monday night we had loads of calls about it and the whole thing was gathering momentum. I had cleared things with Binns' manager, so everything was in place should we do the unexpected."

13 Dec

Stars show up to support Maddren

Bernie is back at the Riverside and this time it's for a get-together to raise awareness and money for the Willie Maddren Motor Neurone Disease Fund. Guest of honour and former Boro player and manager Willie tragically suffers from the disease himself and the likes of Gary Pallister, Stuart Ripley and even Jack Charlton all go along to see him.

Bernie: "When I arrived that night I was one of the first although Willie and his wife Hilary were already there. The first thing I noticed was that Willie had deteriorated since the last time I'd seen him and that saddened me.

"When Pally arrived we both went over and spoke to Willie. He is a lovely guy and we had a great laugh with him. It was a shame his speech had got quite bad but his wife Hilary helped translate his words and it was great to be with him again.

"It's terrible that something like this has happened to a guy like Willie. He's one of the nicest guys you could ever wish to meet and there's not really any other word you can use other than tragic.

"It just shows that in the grand scheme of things it doesn't really matter who you are or how nice you are. You could be the top footballer in the world and the nicest guy but still get struck down with a bad illness."

17 Dec

Slaven and Townsend taken to hospital

It is the week before Christmas and Boro players are visiting various hospitals across Teesside to hand out presents and goodwill messages to children unfortunate enough not to be home over the festive period. Things go well until Boro captain Andy Townsend decides to confront Bernie about one or two comments he's been making on the radio...

Bernie: "I had been saying on the radio that we hadn't been playing attractive football even though I'd said the lads had done an excellent job. The problem is Andy had only listened to the bits after the game and not heard when I'd complimented the lads and, with a bit of spurring on from my mischievous mate Pally, he decided to confront me in the hospital.

"It was all good humoured but all I can still see in my mind is this vision of a poorly boy sitting up in his bed with his arms outstretched waiting for a present, while Andy and I argue over what I have or haven't said on the radio!

"On a more serious note, I've always done visits like that because I think they are so important. I have two kids of my own so it does upset me seeing the sick kids having to spend Christmas in there. It makes you realise how lucky you are and if you can bring a smile to one or two little faces it makes you feel you are doing something useful."

Ali: "Bernie's tiff with Pally was all good spirited but one thing's for sure, it won't change how Bernie is on the radio. He does have strong views and opinions but he's played the game so he's entitled to them, and I think that, on the whole, the players respect him for being like that."

19 and 21 Dec

Bums away! - Manchester United 2 Boro 3

The anticipated day arrives and Bernie starts sweating as Boro amazingly go into a 3-0 lead at Old Trafford. The chants from the Boro fans of 'Bernie, show us your bum' don't help matters but the living legend takes it all in great spirits. United launch a late fightback but it isn't good enough and at the final whistle it is Boro who are victorious and Bernie who is left with a cheeky challenge on his hands two days later in front of a large crowd in Middlesbrough town centre.

Ali: "By the time the Man Utd game came around Bernie's Bum had received a lot of attention so to speak, with the likes of Radio 5 and the national press covering the story.

"At 2-0 up I think Slav was starting to sweat a little bit especially as my commentary at that point went something like 'Gordon has scored and Bernie's bum could be out.' When it went to 3-0 Bernie knew he was well and truly for it. The strange thing is that if you watch a replay of Brian Deane celebrating his goal he swears out loud - just as Bernie did when the ball hit the back of the net!

"I've never known Bernie speechless but he certainly was at the end of that game, he couldn't be for too long though because the world's press wanted to speak to him about what he was going to have to do.

"My next job was to speak to the manager at Binns again to make sure everything was OK. He had fully expected a United win and he sounded like his world had collapsed around him when I said we still wanted to use his shop.

"Two days later we arrived at Binns, as did 3,000 eager fans and the press, all keen to see the living legend's rear end. Someone had lent Bernie a kilt and he had a pair of tasteful red undies on so that he wouldn't shock anyone too much! But before his big moment there was one last thing to do and it was Diane O'Connell from the club's PR Department who landed the thankless task of writing 3-2 on Bernie's behind - one number on each cheek. She certainly wins the Bravest Woman in the World award in my eyes.

"It was like a President's speech in America. There were security guards and people everywhere as Bernie walked towards the window. Then came the moment of truth, and, like the trooper that he is, Bernie lifted his kilt and showed the full moon to the packed high street.

"It was a fantastic occasion and in hindsight it also gave Boro TV some great coverage in the national press. But I'll always remember the day for a comment I overheard from a woman in the crowd that went something like 'that reminds me to stuff the turkey'."

Bernie: *"When Boro were 3-0 up I was absolutely mortified and couldn't believe what I was faced with. I have to admit that when Andy Cole went through one-on-one against Mark Schwarzer I almost wanted him to score to literally save my backside. But time was running out and when Schwarzer saved it I knew I was doomed. Once the game was over I just laughed and wondered whether I'd really have to do it.*

"My answer came when I took my headphones off and heard 3,000 jubilant fans singing 'Bernie show us your bum'. Then when the

national press and radio wanted to interview me about it and it was all over the following day's papers I knew everyone was serious.

"I said in one interview that it was such an achievement that the whole of Teesside should show their backsides in the shop window but when Monday morning came around it was all left to me.

"When we arrived at Binns the manager there had a bit of a sweat on because he didn't quite know what to expect. It got worse as the morning progressed and more and more spectators and members of the world's press arrived for a peak at my behind.

"When the lift doors opened at the bottom of the stairs I couldn't believe it. The crowds in the shop were 20 or 30 deep and they were all cheering me and patting me on the back - it was almost as if I was going to the moon or something!

"So I did the business and hopefully brought a few smiles to a few faces. I enjoyed it, it was great fun but I couldn't help thinking that all the attention I had got had taken something away from the team. Really at the end of the day it should have been them grabbing all the headlines, not me."

26 and 28 Dec

Usual Christmas collapse and handbags at ten paces - Boro 1 Liverpool 3, Derby 2 Boro 1

It's not only the turkey that's stuffed at Christmas, it's usually Boro as well, and this time it was no different as Boro fell victim to both Liverpool at the BT Cellnet Riverside Stadium and Derby at Pride Park. It's a busy time for footballers over the festive period with a few games played over the space of a week, but it's just as busy for those who have to comment on the matches.

Bernie: "I don't know why but ever since I played here we've always had a dodgy spell over the festive period and I can't really put my finger on why. This time around we were absolutely outclassed and outplayed by Liverpool who looked a lot more skilful and pacy and ran out easy winners.

"Then we went to Pride Park and Paulo Wanchope and Dean Sturridge ripped us apart. Again a team showed they had more pace than us and that is what the modern game is all about."

Ali: "For those of us who work in the media and cover football Christmas is a busy time, and to make matters worse it's usually a spell when Boro have an absolute nightmare.

"And this time, after the hype and excitement at Manchester United, was no different. When Bernie was playing we were particularly poor over Christmas and with him you can't put it down to a festive pint or two because he's tee-total.

"I remember the Derby game for one particular reason and that is because I was hit on the head by an irate woman with her handbag. When Mikkel Beck scored the equaliser I put my usual 'calm' interpretation on things and the woman in front of me turned around and gave me a filthy look - but that was nothing compared with what was to come.

"I couldn't believe it. When Derby went to the other end of the field and scored what turned out to be the winning goal she turned round and lashed me round the back of the head with her bag along with a few words that went something like 'take that you noisy sod'. At that point I sensed things were on a bit of a slump."

Jan 2

Rough justice - Man Utd 3 Boro 1

After Boro's stunning win at Old Trafford in the league, revenge is the order of the day in the FA Cup. But controversy is also on the menu as United are awarded a penalty that looks dubious to say the least. It is yet another piece of refereeing that leads to calls from some people for fourth officials to follow games on a monitor at the side of the pitch.

Bernie: *"I said after the win at Old Trafford that I didn't think lightning struck twice and it certainly didn't as United won that game quite easily. The key player for me was Jaap Stam. He had been missing from the league game but this time around he made the Boro strikers look like boys he was so strong and powerful.*

"When Neil Maddison brought down Nicky Butt, straight away I thought it was a penalty, but when I watched it a few times afterwards I wasn't so sure. I didn't think Butt was going to score from where he was anyway so whether it was a penalty or not Maddison was a little bit silly to dive in.

"But it's bad enough having three officials without having four involved. I don't think that would make the game any better or any fairer. The fourth man would still make mistakes and it would lead to unnecessary delays."

Ali: "For me the game illustrated perfectly that technology might have a use in football. Bob Moncur and I have a raging debate about this all the time, but he's so stuck in the past like a dinosaur that he'll never agree to anything along those lines.

"It was disappointing to lose after such a great result in the last game at Old Trafford and without a doubt the key moment was when Nicky Butt went into the area and was challenged by Neil Maddison, with the referee awarding a penalty.

"As soon as he went over both Bernie and I said it was a penalty - it wasn't until we saw a replay afterwards that I realised it wasn't. And of course, to be fair to the referee, like us he only gets one look at the incident. It was a crucial decision that probably cost us the chance of a replay and it really hit home to me that referees should have access to technology to help with decisions like that.

"Some people talk about the delays it would cause but there was a delay anyway as the referee blew his whistle, arguments took place and the penalty area was cleared. Surely in those three or four minutes there was time for a second opinion.

"They should have had cameras in place for a while, the only problem is that if they'd had them in Bernie's day the number of goals he's scored would have been drastically reduced as he'd have been proven offside every time!"

Jan 5

Big Jack

Boro TV has pulled off some scoops in the time it has been on the air but (with the exception of Juninho, arguably) an interview with the legendary Jack Charlton is perhaps the best ever. Bernie knows Big Jack from his Republic of Ireland days and Ali remembers the days the World Cup winner was manager at Ayresome Park so it promises to be a day of nostalgia as well as a cracking interview.

Bernie: *"We all thought it was a very good interview. Jack is a straight guy who has remained very down-to-earth despite all his success. That's what I love the most about him.*

"I've always said you should never change no matter what you achieve and that can certainly be said about Jack. You know his life may have improved financially but as a person he hasn't changed and he still remembers his roots.

"It was great to reminisce with him about our international days together. The thing I remember most about Jack is when I first started training with the Ireland squad. Players like Ray Houghton and Paul McGrath were autographing footballs and I was sat there all shy - believe it or not. Jack asked me if I'd signed them and when I said no he replied 'well f***ing hurry up then because it may be your last time in Ireland'.

"That was his way of getting involved, being one of the lads and helping us enjoy playing the game. Although if you weren't performing he would soon let you know - as I remember him doing vehemently to Tony Cascarino at the 1990 World Cup in Italy.

"The most amazing memory I have of my days with Jack was again in Italy and this time it was when we met the Pope. Along with most of the lads I'm Catholic so it was a big thing for us, but Jack seemed to take it in his stride.

"On the way to the Vatican we were killing ourselves when he said 'what's all the fuss about?'. When we got there the Pope shook Jack's

hand and spoke to him then we all posed for a picture. But the way it came out in the papers was with just me, Jack and the Pope as I was the one stood directly behind the pair of them and they had cut the rest off!"

Ali: "Jack is a legend in the game, a World Cup winner, and when he agreed to do an interview with us we were delighted. He said we could do it at his house but it was a bit strange when he said 'don't forget to bring the fish and chips'.

"Anyway, we turned up but before we had chance to say hello he said 'where's my chips then? I won't do this interview until I've eaten'. So we had to drive all the way into a town to Jack's favourite chippy and get some food before we could begin.

"We went into his kitchen and he said he would warm some plates for us, however, instead of putting them in the oven he used an extremely unusual method - he poured boiling hot water over them and then gave us one each!

"Jack was a really down-to-earth guy. Obviously Bernie remembers him from his Republic days when he used to carry the kit. Apparently he once asked Jack why he took him to the 1990 World Cup and Jack replied 'Bernie, I thought you'd do a good job carrying the bags'.

"The only part of the interview that was a little bit sad was when Jack expressed his disappointment at never being considered for the England manager's role. When the job was up for grabs in the 70s he wrote to the Football Association but he never even received a reply."

Jan 9

"Slav should have played" - Boro 0 Aston Villa 0

The big question in the lead up to the game against Villa is whether or not former Boro star Paul Merson will be at the BT Cellnet Riverside Stadium for the game or not. It is clear an injury will probably prevent him from playing - but would he even turn up at the ground to run the gauntlet of the Boro faithful? As it is the match turns out to be one a certain Mr Slaven would have loved on his day.

Ali: "The build-up to the game was dominated by Merse talk and we'd had loads of letters from fans saying that if there was one game they wanted to win it was that one. But of course Merson didn't even bother to turn up - apparently he was in New York watching a basketball match or something, much to the disappointment of his manager John

Gregory who gave him a well deserved rollicking the following week.

"When he left Boro, Merse came out with all sorts of allegations concerning the players but later on in the season, when he was said to have returned to drinking, it proved that it was he that had the problem and not us. The demons that belong to Paul Merson are nothing to do with Middlesbrough Football Club.

"The Villa game was one that really needed an instinctive finisher to put some of the chances away. Bernie would have loved to play that day - in fact he was claiming on the radio that if he'd been out there he'd have scored at least a hat-trick."

Bernie: *"There was a string of chances that day that all went begging and I was kicking every ball from up in the press box. In my opinion Alun Armstrong is the best instinctive finisher at the club, but of course he was struggling with injury and was missing that day.*

"To be honest there aren't that many predatory strikers in the Premiership these days. The modern game seems to be all about pace and power and a lot of systems the teams play now don't tend to suit the centre-forward. I certainly wouldn't like to play in a 5-3-2 formation week in and week out. In my day I played in a 4-4-2 with players like Stuart Ripley on the wings and that worked well."

Jan 14

Aikido - What's that?

Again it is players' hobbies that are the focus of Boro TV and the cameras roll into Middlesbrough to see what Gianluca Festa does when he's not making tackles out on the pitch. Aikido is Luca's pastime out of work and, after a bit of explaining, Ali soon gets to grips - literally - with what the martial art is all about.

Ali: "Luca had asked me one day at the training ground whether I would go and do a feature on his Aikido class and I said I would - despite not having a clue what the heck Aikido was.

"It turned out that Luca's class was having trouble financially and it was under threat from closure. Some people would have thought that Festa, as a Premiership footballer, could have put his hand in his pocket, and I'm sure he would have if he could, but martial arts have a code of conduct where that is not the done thing.

"But Luca had realised that Boro TV could serve a useful purpose and we later found out our feature and interviews, had helped significantly increase awareness and income for the club, which was great.

"The night itself was enjoyable, albeit a bit painful for me as well. Always game for a laugh I put on one of the white suits that they wear, before a bloke built like a brick outhouse proceeded to swing me around the room like the bulldog does to the cat in cartoons."

Jan 15

Focus on Five Bellies

Paul Gascoigne's long-time friend Jimmy 'Five Bellies' Gardner is the latest interviewee for Bernie. As a fellow prankster, the living legend is looking forward to chatting to Gazza's loyal mate and finding out more about the man who has stood by the midfield maestro throughout his career. But Bernie has a little surprise up his sleeve for Rangers fan Jimmy.

Bernie: "Just as I sat down to do the interview I unbuttoned my shirt to reveal a Celtic top I had hidden underneath. The language that came from Jimmy's mouth was blue to say the least and I'm surprised he agreed to carry on with the interview.

"I've met Jimmy on quite a few occasions and he has a heart of gold the same as Gazza. He was looking well that day but, despite all that, he's still a Rangers fan AND a Geordie - you can't get any worse really can you?

"He told us some stories about Paul and it showed everyone that Gazza's biggest plus is that he has kept the same friends and remembered his background and roots despite all his success.

"The funniest thing Jimmy told me was when I asked him what he does when he opens the front door and is met by the world's paparazzi on his doorstep. He just turned to me and said 'I just turn around and go out the back door'.

"He also revealed the scrutiny he is under every day and told me about the time the press took pictures inside the flat he was selling. I asked him why he let them in and he said he was away at the time and a photographer had posed as a potential buyer to gain access - I couldn't believe how low someone could stoop."

Ali: "Jimmy is very keen on Rangers due to Gazza's time there so of course Bernie, being a massive Celtic fan, decided he would conduct the interview in his Celtic shirt.

"It was good fun and Jimmy was fascinating. He has been with Gazza since he became a professional footballer and he told us some of the things that we never get to find out through the tabloid press, who seem determined to knock him down all the time.

"It also showed how the media circus have not only latched onto Gazza but also Jimmy as well. He told us all about the time he got over his worst fear - heights - and did a charity parachute jump and how all the national papers covered the event."

Jan 16

Bernie is the king - Leeds 2 Boro 0

Boro travel to Elland Road and put in their most disappointing performance of the season to date. But there is double joy for Middlesbrough-born Leeds star Jonathan Woodgate who not only celebrates a win for his side but also gets to meet his lifelong idol - one Bernie Slaven!

Ali: "Woodgate wasn't playing that day, he was doing commentary for a local radio station, but his hero is Bernie, and instead of speaking when he should have been he spent the entire game looking along the press box at the Living Legend.

"At half-time Woodgate was trying to track down Bernie for his autograph, without success. But by the end of the game he made sure he got what he wanted, along with a firm handshake. It did Bernie's ego no end of good!

"We also took our cameras to Elland Road to follow the Middlesbrough Disabled Supporters' Club and show how they get to away games. They are tremendous people who, despite their disabilities, are dedicated to the Boro, but the problem is that their coach looks like something that was previously drawn by two horses. They are raising funds to buy a new one and we went along to lend our help and hopefully boost the kitty a little bit. ntl also agreed to double the money when they reached £5,000 and that target has been achieved."

Bernie: *"We got absolutely battered off the park that day and at one point I remember saying to Ali that if Robbo didn't change things then we were going to get beat by four or five. Thankfully we managed to keep it down to two but I'm amazed it wasn't more.*

"I remember seeing Woodgate that day but what opened my eyes even more was an article I read in the programme which had quotes from another young Leeds player, Lee Matthews, who is also from Middlesbrough. I couldn't believe what I was seeing. There in front of me was a whole page under the headline 'Bernie is the king' which said how Matthews used to watch me from the Holgate End and thought I was the best. It made me feel old but at the same time I was thinking I

must have done something right to have two young players at Leeds, who have become a very good side, saying that I'm their hero."

Jan 17

Fly me to the moon - Boro TV meets Mogga

Ali and Bernie go to interview former Boro defender Tony Mowbray - the man Bruce Rioch once said he would take with him if he flew to the moon. It is a particularly nostalgic day as Mogga was Bernie's captain when he was at Boro and Ali can remember many an impressive performance from the solid centre-half.

Bernie: "We met up with Mogga in a hotel and had a good chat about his time at Boro and Celtic, which of course I was interested in. He's a nice guy who was a great servant to Middlesbrough. The interview was quite a poignant one and put life into perspective for me because we also spoke about his wife, who sadly died from cancer during his time in Glasgow.

"I've never quite got the grasp of what Bruce meant when he said he'd take Mogga to the moon but I joked to him that sometimes I wish the pair of them had gone there!"

Ali: "Mogga came into the team as a young kid under Malcolm Allison and later led the team forward under Bruce Rioch. He did so much for the club so it was great to speak to him.

"I remember playing against Newport one year at a little old ground that resembled a shed and Mowbray strolled up the pitch in the last minute before despatching a bullet header into the top corner of the net to win the game 1-0.

"Then there's the game that most people remember, when we were going for promotion to the top flight and we played Aston Villa (1988). I can still picture him now diving to head the ball into the back of the net with six minutes remaining to win the game 2-1."

Jan 28

Dress rehearsal

Throughout the season the Boro Brain competition has been trying to find the fan who knows the most about their favourite club. So to the final, and if Ali can get his timekeeping right, a

winner will be found. Also to be announced at an exciting night at the Tall Trees Hotel is the winner of the Boro dress competition after students from a local college were challenged to design the ultimate in Boro fashion wear. The whole night is to be covered live on Boro TV.

Ali: "It was an interesting night because it was the first time we'd done a live outside broadcast from anywhere. Up until that point it had always been put together in the studio.

"We had finalists for both the Boro Brain competition and the dress designing and the night itself went down really well but it just showed the effort you have to go to when you are putting out something live. We had to hire a big truck, called a link truck, which beams the programme up to the atmosphere and back down again into people's homes - something Bernie was absolutely baffled by.

"Everything went brilliantly except for when the battery went flat in my ear piece. Because of that I couldn't hear a word the producer was saying to me and I had to blag my way through. But all in all everything went well and we managed to keep Bernie away from the sauna."

Bernie: *"I thought the evening went very well for what was our first live show although for me there was a bit too much talk about dresses and not enough about football.*

"At the end of the night I got asked some questions about myself by Boro historian Harry Glasper and boy were some of them tough. But I got most of them right and, as I was being sponsored for each correct answer, raised around £800 for charity."

Jan 30

Gordon for England - Boro 0 Leicester City 0

A drab 0-0 draw is on the cards but the papers over the following days are full of praise for in-form wing-back Dean Gordon. They call for him to be considered in the England set-up and Bernie and Ali also back calls for Gordon to play for his country.

Bernie: *"I can't really remember that game - that tells you it most have been a real cracker! All I can recall is the form of Dean Gordon at that time. As an attacking wing-back he was on fire and was certainly causing problems for opposition defences. I think next season will be a massive test for him and if he can carry on performing as well he should be pushing for an England place."*

Ali: "The month of January just showed for me how we can have a spell where we do really well for features and interviews on Boro TV and the football can become almost incidental. Bernie and I hardly had a breather and the time to watch a match in January - and then we did get chance we weren't treated to too much.

"The only bright thing that did come out of it was the form of Dean Gordon. When you look at the left-backs in the country at that time I don't think there was anyone playing better and I can't help thinking that if he'd been playing for a Man Utd or an Arsenal he'd have been in the England squad."

Feb 4

Custard pie capers

The 'will he/won't he' Juninho saga is finally laid to rest when the little man decides he is going to stay with Atletico Madrid at least until the end of the season. The news delights Bernie who has made his views about the Brazilian perfectly clear and he celebrates in style with a little surprise for Ali.

Ali: "Everybody had been so hopeful that Juninho was coming and when it all fell through I decided it would be good to pack away all my Juninho memories, such as posters and goodies, in a box on Boro TV.

"Bernie had put another box on set which had written on it 'To Ali and everyone on Teesside. Regards Madrid'. I kept asking what was in the box but he just kept saying he'd tell me later.

"Right at the end of the show, my curiosity got the better of me and I asked him again. This time he put his hand in the box, pulled out a great big custard pie and promptly slammed it in my face. It went everywhere - all over my shirt and trousers. It was time to plot my revenge."

Bernie: *"We decided to give Ali a little surprise to finally bring the Juninho thing to an end so we bought the huge custard pie and I put it in a box so he would have no idea what was going on.*

"He was curious and asked me throughout the programme what was in the box so finally I told him to close his eyes and right on cue I pushed the pie right into his face. It went everywhere - up his nose and all over his nice new shirt and trousers.

"It was just a bit of fun. Ali's always game for a laugh, and although it made me look like the bad guy, we all knew it was in good humour. I think I got to do something that half of Teesside would love to do to Ali!"

Feb 5

Passionate Pollock

Bernie's latest job is to interview former Boro midfielder Jamie Pollock and it turns into an interesting one as he looks back at his time at the club and gives his frank views about one or two of his foreign team-mates. Despite being at Manchester City it is clear that honest Jamie's heart still belongs on Teesside and this delights the living legend.

Bernie: "It was a great interview and it was just typical Jamie as he had a go at some of the foreigners who were at Boro when he was here and said how much he loves Boro.

"Jamie wore his heart on his sleeve when he played and he still does. He's still a massive Boro fan like me so it was nice to talk to him. It was great to hear because in all the interviews I've done I haven't talked to many guys who have that much passion and at the same time it must have been great for the fans to see on Boro TV."

Feb 6

Bernie gets wound up & Ali gets revenge - Liverpool 3 Boro 1

Boro's New Year slump continues as they are ripped apart at Anfield and boss Bryan Robson is none too pleased with the performance of his players. However, he's not the only one full of hell when it comes to the Century Radio phone-in after the game. The living legend becomes the livid legend as he lets rip into one or two callers - while Ali sits beside him with a guilty grin on his face.

Ali: "The Juninho thing had all gone pear-shaped. I had decided that it was time to wind Bernie up big time and I thought the journey to Anfield would be the perfect time to do it.

"On the way I told him that our bosses had been bombarded with letters complaining about his negative stance on Juninho and that he had to tow the line otherwise it could be the end of the line for me and him on the airwaves.

"He immediately went off on one and started saying things like 'no-one's going to censor me' and we had a great phone-in that night after what was a disappointing game when Bernie was really up for it and giving full-blooded answers to every question. The great thing about Bernie is that all you have to do is ignite the flame a little bit, then just sit back and watch him explode."

Bernie: "In the car on the way to Anfield Ali wound me up by telling me that we had received a stack of letters and e-mails complaining about my views on Juninho - it later turned out that there'd been one letter.

"I told him that I didn't care what people said because it was only my opinions. I said I might be wrong on certain things but they are my

feelings. I would certainly never be a yes man and that if people wanted me to go then I would.

"I was well and truly on my high horse and completely unaware that Ali was winding me up. But it got me fired up for the commentary and on the way home he admitted that he had been having me on - as if the result wasn't bad enough!"

Feb 8

It's history

History is the theme as Boro TV's continuing search for a wide variety of features takes them on the trail of Boro's old grounds. Over a period of a couple of weeks, Bernie and Ali visit all of the club's previous 'stadia' culminating in an amusing trip to the site of the legendary Ayresome Park.

Ali: "After doing a bit of research we visited all of Boro's old grounds but first we found the Talbot Hotel which was supposedly the meeting place for a tripe supper, from which Middlesbrough Football Club was formed. That story later turned out to be a load of tripe in itself but it was interesting.

"We had a chat with a guy called Paul Stephenson who has written a book on the pubs and clubs in Middlesbrough. We then thought it would be good to go to Middlesbrough Library to try and find Paul's book - but that plan backfired when we got thrown out of the library for making too much noise!

"After that we went to Albert Park, where Boro also used to play. We had had special moustaches made to make us look like old fashioned footballers and we spent the afternoon dribbling the ball in and out of the dog muck.

"In later weeks we did great features at the former Breckon Road and Linthorpe Road grounds before capping it all off with a hilarious piece with Bernie and Gary Gill at the housing estate that now stands on the site of Ayresome Park.

"That day we proved Bernie really can score a penalty, following the infamous incident against Ipswich in 1992 when he blazed the ball into the Holgate End from the spot with the final kick of the game."

Bernie: *"I had heard a story years ago about a Boro youth player called Tony Matthana who had caught his finger on a crossbar hook whilst putting up the nets one day and ripped it clean off.*

"Amazingly when we went along to the Talbot Hotel we discovered that he was the publican there so we had a good chat with him about the accident and the good old days when he almost made it into the Boro first team.

"For the final sketch we went to the houses where Ayresome Park was and Gilly and I pretended that we lived next door to each other to give the piece a bit of humour. Ali then came and knocked on both doors and the idea was that he was supposed to act like he was surprised to see us both living there. But I decided to give him a genuine surprise by stripping off - and he was absolutely stunned when I opened the front door wearing nothing but my smalls."

Feb 9

Bloody Scunthorpe

Boro take on Scunthorpe in an FA Cup Youth tie at the BT Cellnet Riverside Stadium and again there is a prime example of how big a part football plays in Ali's life. The day is also his eldest daughter's 14th birthday and he has promised to meet up with her and her friends after the game to celebrate the occasion - until the unexpected happens that is.

Ali: "We had decided we wanted to cover the game because it is such a prestigious trophy. I had said that I would then meet up with my daughter in the restaurant straight after the match, just in time to see her cut her cake. Then lo and behold, in the final seconds of the game, Scunthorpe equalised to take the game into extra-time and I had to stay at the Riverside for an extra half hour.

"I got to the restaurant as my daughter and her friends were just walking out of the door and I had to make a grovelling apology, although I think she's forgiven me now. And of all the teams to ruin such a special occasion - bloody Scunthorpe!"

Feb 11

It's a lock-out

Following prankster Bernie's custard pie antics, Ali gets a second slice of revenge when the living legend turns up to film Boro TV at the Stockton studio. His usual extravagant arrival, complete with lights flashing and horns sounding, soon fizzles out as the

former star striker realises getting into the building might prove a little more difficult than usual.

Bernie: *"I turned up for work that day, got out of my car and showed the security man my pass as usual. I couldn't believe it when he turned round and said I was not allowed into the building on the orders of Mr Brownlee. So I went to the reception area and low and behold I was told that my pass had been stopped. I got straight on the phone and spoke to the boss but he refused point blank to budge.*

"But it was just another sketch for television and I don't mind really because it made Ali look like the baddie again. We've done a fair few pieces like that now and our acting is getting so much better that I think we're being lined up for roles in Coronation Street!"

Ali: "The Living Legend turned up and we pretended that his pass to come in had been revoked. He was full of hell as he couldn't believe it and his language was on the blue side to say the least.

"Then he proceeded to whack a football at the window in a desperate attempt to get some attention before storming into the boss's office, slamming the door and demanding to know what was going on before he eventually conceded that he'd been stitched up.

"We showed it all on the show and it was just like watching Laurel and Hardy. The final clip was brilliant as we saw Bernie apologising for hitting me with the pie - but as he walked off the last shot was of him with another custard pie behind his back."

Feb 15

The icing on the cake

Boro TV pay a visit to the Rockliffe Park training complex to see Bryan Robson in the week where the popular programme is celebrating it's first birthday. And to celebrate in style, Ali has a little surprise up his sleeve for the Boro boss - and he brings translator Zelia Knight in on the act. Things go well until Zelia gets a little over-excited at being on television.

Ali: "To celebrate we decided to get a cake with a number one on it but the only cake I could find in time was one that had a load of icing sugar on the top. Anyway, what followed was like something from a Terry Thomas sketch. I thought it would be no use if I sat through the whole interview with a cake on my lap so I asked Zelia if she could come in after about ten minutes and present it to Robbo.

"We went into Robbo's office and barely had we sat down when Zelia opened the door. I managed to politely usher her away and ask her to come back in ten but believe it or not she was back within about a minute.

"Again I managed to get rid of her but not only was Bryan getting a bit suspicious but I could also see that she'd lit the candle on the cake and it was virtually down to it's last embers.

"Anyway, when the door opened for a third time I decided we had best get on with things as the flame had almost flickered out. So Zelia presented Robbo with the cake and everything looked set to return to normal.

"Then the unthinkable happened as Zelia turned to Bryan and asked him if he wanted to blow the candle out. He of course obliged - and proceeded to blast about half a kilo of icing sugar all over his plush new office!"

Feb 16

Focus on Keith Lamb

As part of the continuing search to talk to people from throughout the whole of Middlesbrough Football Club Bernie heads to the helm for an interview with Chief Executive Keith Lamb.

Bernie: "I know Keith from my days as a player but back then it would just be a case of saying 'hello' to him because I didn't have much to do with the management and directors. So it did seem a bit strange to have to sit down and talk to him at length. It turned out to be a good interview as Keith told us about his role at the club and what he is involved in on a day-to-day basis.

"It highlighted again just how much football has changed. Keith has a high pressure job and a lot of decisions to make and at the modern-day Boro he is no longer in charge of a small club, instead he's at the helm of a massive company."

Feb 17

Good old Goodison - Everton 5 Boro 0

Goodison Park doesn't hold particularly good memories for Ali and Bernie and this trip is no different as Boro crash to a 5-0

defeat - their worst of the season so far. It is one of those days where things go wrong right from the start, I mean if you can't even get into the press box what chance have you got?

Bernie: *"The first person I bumped into was former Liverpool star Jan Molby who is also a radio commentator now he's stopped playing. He said hello which surprised me as I didn't think he knew who I was.*

"He went on to tell me that loads of Liverpool fans had been pestering him to show his behind in a local shop window and that was when it really hit home that my exploits in Binns window really had been seen much further afield than Teesside."

Ali: "From the minute I opened the press box door at Goodison I could see it was packed to the rafters and what made things worse was that Jan Molby was sat right at the end of one of the rows and he's built like a brick outhouse.

"We got absolutely whacked 5-0 by a side that were much better on the night but, just when we thought things couldn't get any worse, we couldn't remember where we'd parked the car and it took us ages to find it.

"One amusing thing though was the story we heard about two nosy Everton stewards who'd been listening to Robbo telling his players off after the game right outside the dressing room. Halfway through, someone opened the door and they promptly fell in!"

Bernie: *"On the way home from Everton we stopped for a Chinese meal but as I couldn't manage to finish my egg-fu-yung I decided it would be funny to pour the remainder into Ali's equipment bag.*

"I completely forgot I had done it and it wasn't until a few days later, after a strange smell had been reported throughout the building at ntl, that I had to admit what I had done.

"It reminded me of a couple of things I did as a player firstly when I put a fish in Gary Gill's bag and then when I put a giant crab in Stuart Ripley's bed. However Gilly did get me back by putting horse manure in my bag.

"But the best food story came after I had enjoyed a night out with Curtis Fleming and we stopped to get a bite to eat. Curtis plumped for a kebab, which he left - unwrapped - on the dashboard of my car whilst he went to order a Kentucky Fried Chicken for me.

"Meanwhile, I found a space to park in but as I reversed the kebab toppled onto the floor, picking up loads of dog hairs and bits of chocolate on the way. In my panic I just picked it up, put the wrapper back on and put it back on the dashboard.

"Curtis returned soon after and after handing over my food, he immediately got stuck into his. At one point he did complain that his kebab tasted a bit chocolatey but he finished every last morsel of it - dog hairs and all!"

Feb 20

We'd better watch out - Boro 0 Spurs 0

A third consecutive 0-0 home draw sees Boro slip further down the table and almost sends Bernie and Ali to sleep halfway through their live radio commentary. But the living legend has more pressing things on his mind as he gears up for a night at Newcastle Arena where he is due to meet one of the giants of modern day pop music.

Bernie: *"We had arranged to go and see Robbie Williams in Newcastle that night and we had backstage passes thanks to a colleague who has done work with Robbie. We were all looking forward to it after what was a snore draw that afternoon.*

"We got to the Arena that night and although we missed the first couple of songs after haggling over our tickets with security outside, we enjoyed a fantastic concert along with my mate Pally and Gazza who were also there. Afterwards we went backstage but I only got to speak to Robbie briefly because everyone was clamouring to have a word with him or get his autograph.

"Robbie is a fan of another one of my old clubs Port Vale and I had heard that I was one of his idols because I scored for them at Wembley. That may or may not be true but I had also heard a rumour that he wants to buy Port Vale and it would have been nice to ask him about both things - maybe next time!"

Ali: "The Spurs game just showed how funny football can be and how easily things can spiral downwards. At Christmas if we he had beaten Liverpool we would have gone to second in the table yet just two months later a bit of a slump had set in.

"Along with the rest of the Boro fans I certainly didn't want to go back down again but, after what was another lacklustre performance, it was looking like we could get sucked into a relegation battle again."

Happy birthday and Happy Easter

The cameras are back at the BT Cellnet Riverside Stadium, this time to focus on the first birthday of the highly successful Willie Maddren Education Centre which is housed within the ntl East Stand. It is also the launch of Boro's Easter Egg appeal where chocolate is donated by local people and firms and then handed out to children who are unfortunate enough to be poorly and hospital-bound over the Easter period. Other than Bernie and Ali, there are one or two other familiar faces - in the shape of Bryan Robson and Paul Gascoigne - helping celebrate both things.

Ali: "Again we saw the side of Gazza that we all know and love. We saw that he is really comfortable when put in a room with a group of kids and that when he is in that kind of environment how brilliant he is.

"We did an interview with him and former referee George Courtney, who is in charge of the Willie Maddren Centre as part of his job as Boro's Director of Community Initiatives, to try and get the angle that Gazza was there helping out the man who used to run around the pitch booking him.

"And Gazza proved again that he's still the one person all the youngsters want to see and meet and not the fading star that some people and sections of the press make him out to be. It's true that if you go and ask Bernie's young son Dominic who his favourite player is he'll say Gazza - despite his dad keep trying to tell him that he was actually a better player!"

Bernie: *"My son Dominic is a big Boro fan and his favourite player is most definitely Paul Gascoigne. But before that it was Ravanelli so I for one am delighted that he's now changed to Gazza!"*

Feb 27

When the going gets tough - Sheffield Wednesday 3 Boro 1

Things aren't getting any better out on the pitch and a visit to Hillsborough ends in a crushing defeat. Ali starts to worry about the way things are going, as do the fans who flood the radio

phone-in after the game with their views on how to stop the rot.

Bernie: *"We were torn apart, particularly on the left-hand side by Peter Rudi and Andy Hinchcliffe who both had excellent games. Benito Carbone was a constant threat and I thought he was tremendous. even though some of the home fans were saying he was only average that day.*

"Following the match, the phone-in clearly showed that people were getting worried about the poor run of form and that things needed to turn around pretty sharpish. A lot of callers were worried that we were about to get sucked into a relegation battle again."

Ali: "After the game we had a lot of fans call in and the general consensus was that the bad run had to stop. And I had to agree because, like many others I enjoy the rollercoaster ride that is being a Boro fan, but I like the ups better than the downs."

Feb 28

Bernie on the run

The day has come for Bernie to swap his studio gear for running shorts as he has agreed to run the Redcar half-marathon to raise money for charity. Always game for a laugh, the living legend is as determined to take things in his stride as Ali is to get hilarious footage of the former footballer on the run. But things don't go exactly to plan for the ex-Boro star.

Ali: "In a bid to try and lift the depressing run of form, and to raise some money for charity, Bernie had stupidly agreed to run the Redcar half-marathon - something that we all thought was hilarious.

"Bernie was well prepared for the race having run all the way home to his house in Middlesbrough from Redcar the week before, so we decided to take the cameras along so that Boro TV viewers could share our enjoyment of watching him sweat.

"On the day Bernie came trotting confidently up to the starting line - well he thought it was - full of bravado. Well he was until he found out he was half a mile away from the starting pistol. So an angry looking living legend jogged off in the right direction, but low and behold as he got onto a bridge overlooking the start, the klaxon sounded and the rest of the runners set off - not the best of starts by anyone's standards.

"Bernie did brilliantly to complete the race and raised a good sum for charity. We stopped at different points on the course to record him running past but I have to say the language from the lips of the living legend when he saw me lying down at the 11 mile stage with a refreshing ice cream was a little bit blue to say the least!"

Bernie: *"Whilst I was out a few months earlier I had bumped into a woman who had said she was running the half-marathon for charity and could I do anything to help. So I decided I would do it as well and roped my old team-mate Mark Proctor into running with me.*

"To practice I had done a ten mile road run a week earlier and, although it left me drained both physically and mentally, it made me realise that the challenge was something I could complete. I enjoyed the early part of the race but both Proc and I were exhausted by the time we got to the ten mile marker. Ironically my race number was 999. I think that was so I could call an ambulance if I collapsed.

"By the time I got to Ali, who was taking the mickey out of me at the 11 mile marker, I was in no mood for joking and in fact had I had the energy to lift my leg I would have directed a left-footer in his direction!

"Proc and I were absolutely knackered by the time we crossed the finishing line but the most important thing is that we managed to raise a good few quid for charity. Now we are in training for the London Marathon which we have decided to do next year - we must be mad."

Mar 1

Bernie meets Archie

The Living Legend meets up with his old Boro team-mate Archie Stephens in Great Ayton. He enjoys his chat with the player, who was the first of his many strike partners at Ayresome Park, but also a man who was capable of springing the odd surprise off the pitch.

Bernie: *"I remember the time when I was at Boro and we travelled to Lilleshall for some fitness training and, for whatever reason, I had to room with Archie, even though I usually shared with my mate Pally.*

"At one point I left the room to go and get a drink and when I returned I couldn't see him for a cloud of smoke. It turned out the great Archie Stephens was a big puffer - yes, I said puffer!

"He was one of the few professional players I ever saw that smoked, but he couldn't half play as well. He had terrific aerial power so we used to say to him 'don't put the boots on your feet, put them on your head'.

"He is a typical Liverpudlian with a great sense of humour and I enjoyed the interview because it showed he hadn't changed. He still had the cheek - in fact the first thing he asked me was if I could get him any tickets for the forthcoming Chelsea game."

Mar 2

Camera capers - Rangers 4 Boro 4

The Boro TV team travel to Glasgow to see Boro take part in former Rangers star Alan McLaren's testimonial. It is yet another journey back home for the living legend and Ali decides it would be fun to trace his sidekick's roots. But the day is soon to be ruined by a little bit of Scottish weather.

Ali: "We travelled to Scotland early because we wanted to do a feature on Bernie's roots - not his hair, but where he comes from! So we decided to go the home of Albion Rovers, which was the last team Bernie played for in Scotland.

"We recreated the walk from the train station to the ground - in those days Bernie was too poor to have a personalised Mercedes - and when we got there we found that amazingly the kitman there was the same bloke who Bernie had known previously.

"With all due respect, the ground itself was just about up to Northern

League standards and it made me realise how far Bernie went in the game to go from there to becoming a legend at Middlesbrough. But what should have been a great little piece ended in a bit of disaster as the pouring rain damaged the camera. We did all we could to try and dry it out but in the end we had to give up and stop recording.

"Later we went to Ibrox, which Bernie wasn't too keen on doing being a massive Celtic fan, and enjoyed watching a brilliant goal from Paraguayan trialist Miguel Dominguez. But, again, we couldn't do any filming."

Bernie: *"It was great to go back to Glasgow again but it was just disappointing it was Rangers and not Celtic. It was also nice to go back to Albion but I have to admit it was a surprise to see that old Jimmy, the kitman, was there.*

"The game that night was quite entertaining and the goal by Dominguez was out of this world. It was the kind of individual effort that, if it had been scored by Juninho, would have been raved about for years to come.

"If I ever go back home with anyone else I always take them to eat at my favourite curry house so that night, although Ali was banking on haggis, he actually ended up with a fiery Vindaloo. The place must be good because they've even got a picture up on the wall of that really famous Scottish person - Lorraine Kelly! - eating there. I must be due to have my face put up there alongside hers by now."

Mar 3

Bernie gets his kit off - again!

By now Bernie's bum is as well known on Teesside as the man himself but, ever the exhibitionist, the Living Legend is back showing off his body as he helps launch the search for Boro's new away kit. The club has decided that the fans will choose their favourite strip and Bernie is brought in to the BT Cellnet Riverside Stadium to model the new designs.

Ali: "We had already had plenty of chances to see Bernie's backside as everyone will know but this time it was his chest that was on display and it certainly shocked the female photographer that was there on the day.

"As a humorous piece for Boro TV we had decided that after he had modelled each one of the four designs he would wear one of his own - just his incredibly hairy chest. It was just a prank but the photographer seemed shocked and Bernie being Bernie just turned round and said 'what's the matter, have you not seen a man's body before?' I'm sure Bernie was a stripper in a previous life!"

Bernie: *"It was just one of my pranks and little did I know that when we showed the feature on Boro TV they didn't edit out the pictures of me without a shirt on. It was funny the way it was done.*

"But what it does mean is that, following the Binns episode as well, the people of Teesside have seen most of my body and it could get worse as I have said on radio that I'll strip totally if we win the league."

Mar 4

Swimming lessons with the living legend

Super-fit Bernie enjoys nothing more than a daily swim and he has become known as a regular visitor at the Neptune Centre in Middlesbrough. To prove the point he invites the Boro TV cameras along to film him and his mates in the baths - with a little help from a couple of elderly gentlemen who are determined to get in on the act.

Bernie: *"We decided it would be great fun to show what I do every morning so we all got up at the crack of dawn and went down to the Neptune Centre to see me and my mates in action.*

"We had a good old time and I even got a few of the old dears to sing a song in the middle of the pool, but unfortunately it was never shown on Boro TV which was a shame because it was very funny."

Ali: "Seeing Bernie swim was good for a laugh but the footage never made it onto screen. I realised he never ever gets his hair wet because he just walks up and down the pool with it above the water.

"And, completely out of the blue, these two old blokes decided it was time for their three minutes of fame and started singing 'always look on the bright side of life' in the middle of the pool!"

Rioch replies

Once he is towelled off Bernie faces one of his most nervy interviews ever as he goes along to speak to his former boss at the Boro, Bruce Rioch. The nerves are there due to the immense respect he has for a man who was very popular with his players

despite ruling with a rod of iron at times. But he has no need to worry as the interview turns into another cracker.

Bernie: *"When I met up with Bruce he unexpectedly gave me a big hug as if we were best friends who hadn't seen each other for an eternity . It was good to see him again and have the chance to talk to him as he is a man I have a great deal of respect for.*

"The interview went on for over two hours, which is the longest yet, and even when the cameras were turned off we spent a lot more time talking off the record. He is a very clever man who is just so interesting to listen to as he knows so many tales.

"I have always rated him as a top man. I always knew he would go to the top of the management ladder, and he did that with Arsenal, because he is disciplined and knows how to command respect.

"I remember one time when I was playing with him and he produced this long list of things he said I needed to do to improve my game. There was so much there I began to think I couldn't play at all. But it was just his style of man management. It was his way of getting to players and winding you up so that you were certain to produce the goods."

Ali: "Bruce was Bernie's big mentor. He was the manager who he really had respect for and the only man yet who's ever got him to have a shave of a morning - it was probably the fear factor at work as Bruce would fine anyone with stubble!

"To meet up with and interview someone who you have so much admiration for yet haven't worked with for around 10 years is quite difficult but it went well and Bruce recalled some great tales.

"I remember Bruce's style quite well. I recall the time Trevor Senior signed for £200,000 and then had a nightmare game on his debut. Bruce was irate and instead of doing the post-match press conference himself as usual, he sent Senior to talk to us!

"Bruce was a great manager and I'm sure many other Boro fans agree the Rioch years were some of the best we've ever had. I'll always remember the reception the team got when we won promotion to the First Division and there were people hanging off the lamp-posts outside the Town Hall."

Mar 5

Deane goes to Port

Boro striker Brian Deane heads for Port Clarence to help present

prizes to children at a local school as part of a crime prevention scheme. He is closely followed by the Boro TV cameras.

Ali: "We picked up our very own Mr Jinx from the stadium and headed for Port Clarence although we had to explain on the way that we weren't quite going to a fishing village as he had thought.

"Everything went really well at the school and the kids were delighted to see Brian. There was a funny moment when Brian chose the winner of a badge designing competition only to pick the one kid in the school who didn't support Boro - he was a Manchester United fan!

"Joking aside, it really was a worthwhile day because there you had a case of children in an area which does have one or two problems receiving a welcome boost thanks to the visit of a footballer."

Mar 14

Back on track - Boro 3 Southampton 0

A great result is the order of the day as Boro get back to winning ways. Super centre-back Steve Vickers wraps up the result with a stunning strike. The goal comes as a bit of a shock to many fans who are not used to the defender getting himself on the scoresheet but some commentators are not surprised in the slightest.

Ali: "I always have a little flutter on Steve Vickers to score the first goal, so of course I was gutted that he weighed in with the last one because once again I didn't win a thing. But the result helped lift a huge cloud that seemed to have been hanging over the club since the great Old Trafford win in December. Had we lost or drawn that day the chances are we would have been drawn into a relegation dogfight.

"Steve's strike was a thunder volley which to most people was absolutely unheard of but I always remember when we played Tranmere a few years ago and he stepped up and scored with a 30 yard free-kick - so I wasn't as surprised as many of the fans!"

Bernie: *"I was really pleased to see Steve score that day because he comes in for quite a bit of stick at times from some of the fans. And most of it is unjustified because you don't play as many league games as he has in his career if you aren't a decent player.*

"After the Sheffield Wednesday away game, we had callers saying how poor they thought Vickers was when in fact he was the best of the three centre-backs. Sometimes I wonder which game these people were at.

"When you are a defender and you start getting stick it's hard to get away from it. But it's different if you are a striker, because if guys like myself are having a hard time, we only need to put the ball in the back of the net and everyone loves us again."

Mar 15

Off to Darlo

Bernie travels up the road to Darlington, not because he's changed their allegiances, but to interview Boro old boy David Hodgson who is the Quakers' boss. He is happy to talk to Boro TV and Bernie even finds out something interesting about his old goal celebrations.

Bernie: "David is an all-round nice guy who was good to talk to but the biggest surprise I got was when I asked him what his most vivid memory of Ayresome Park was. I couldn't believe it when he turned around and said he'd never forget the way I used to jump on the Holgate End fence after I'd scored a goal. I thought he was just taking the mickey at first but it turned out he was deadly serious.

"Another interesting thing Hodgy said was that he genuinely enjoys being a manager more than being a player. I've never heard anyone say that before and I'll probably never hear it again. I've never been a manager but I certainly can't imagine anything being like the thrill of actually being out there on the pitch. A few days later I sent a letter thanking him for the interview - and enclosed a photo of myself jumping on the Holgate End!"

Mar 17

Thank youth

Having missed his daughter's birthday celebrations just weeks before due to Boro's exploits in the FA Youth Cup Ali has mixed feelings when the side are dumped out of the competition in a replay by local rivals Newcastle. As a massive Boro fan he is keen to see his team do well at all levels but at the same time there's only so many hours in a week and they need to be divided between work and home life.

Ali: "It was the end of the road for the youth team that night and as a fan naturally I was upset but I didn't shed too many tears after how the

FA Youth Cup had affected my daughter's celebrations shortly before. But from a professional point of view we were all disappointed as plans were in place to cover the next round live on Boro TV."

Mar 19

O'Neill on the run

With transfer deadline day looming, Robbo swoops to sign long-term target Keith O'Neill from Norwich for just £700,000. From the off Ali and Bernie witness at first hand the winger's wicked sense of humour and find out exactly what former Boro boss turned Canaries gaffer Bruce Rioch gave O'Neill as a leaving present.

Ali: "Bernie had returned from his interview with Rioch two weeks earlier saying how his mentor had changed and mellowed out at Norwich. But after speaking to O'Neill, I realised how the Living Legend couldn't have been further from the truth.

"Apparently the day before Keith had signed on the dotted line to come to Boro, Bruce had very kindly told Keith he was going to give him something to remember him by - and sent him out on a five mile run. Deep down he's definitely the same old Bruce.

"The arrival of Keith at that time was exactly what the club needed. In walked this bubbly, funny Irishman who always has a smile on his face and he gave all the other players a lift - as well as one or two of his opponents out on the pitch!"

Bernie: *"The signing of Keith O'Neill came at a great time for everyone at Boro because he has the kind of infectious personality that is brilliant to have around the place and rubs off on people around him. He was like a breath of fresh air and straight away he was getting people rattled. I know that even when he's not in the team he's still the one player in the dressing room before the game who's shouting encouragement and psyching everyone up.*

"I honestly thought Rioch had chilled out a bit after my talk with him a couple of weeks before but when Keith told me he had made him run five miles as a leaving present I knew he was still the same old gaffer."

Mar 20

Revenge is sweet - Nottingham Forest 1 Boro 2

A year on from a 4-0 drubbing at the City Ground, Boro return to the Midlands and gain sweet revenge thanks to a classy last gasp winner from striker Brian Deane. However, Bernie bumps into former Forest defender turned commentator Larry Lloyd at the stadium and there's a little bit of confusion as to whether or not the pair had ever played against each other before.

Bernie: *"We bumped into Larry Lloyd that day and Ali, with his vast football knowledge, asked him what it was like to mark me - even though the pair of us knew we had never played against each other at all during our careers. But Larry has a great sense of humour and instead of just fobbing Ali off he just looked inside the top pocket of his shirt and said 'if I'd played against Bernie he'd be in here'.*

"It was a good result that day and a fine goal from Brian Deane, who is another player who has had his fair share of stick. However he proved that day the qualities he has as we got revenge from the previous season."

Ali: "The season had continued to tick over but it was great to get a win under our belts against a side who had thrashed us on the way to their title the previous season.

"On a general note, it is worth saying that it certainly makes travelling to long distance away games much more fun if you can come away at the end of the day with three points."

Mar 22

Coops and Ali go back to school

To help celebrate National Book Week, Boro defender Colin Cooper heads for a Darlington school to read a story to a group of eager kids. Ali is not far behind him with a camera crew in tow and he's impressed with how Coops has planned - with a little bit of help from home - for his meeting with the youngsters.

Ali: "Despite having a pretty bad bout of flu, Coops was brilliant. Instead of just going along and picking up any old book he had consulted his own kids beforehand and asked them which story they thought he should read.

"So, full of a cold, he turned up with his copy of Snow White and the

Seven Dwarfs and read the story. It was good to see that as a family person himself, he obviously recognised the importance of reading, especially for the younger generation, and he went down really well with all the children."

Mar 28

The little man returns - Boro 1 Atletico Madrid 1

Following all the speculation surrounding Juninho and a possible return to Boro the great news is that the little man is back at the BT Cellnet Riverside Stadium - but only for a friendly against his team, Atletico Madrid. Over 17,000 fans turn out to see his return but the game ends up being something of an anti-climax in the eyes of Ali and Bernie.

Ali: "We had been preparing all week for the game in the hope that we'd be able to get another chat with Juninho following our visit to see him in Madrid. However, just a few days before, I was close to not being around to see the little man at all, thanks to Boro's physio, Bob Ward.

"He had very kindly let me have a look around the state-of-the-art equipment he uses at the training ground and had let me have a go on a running machine that looks like something out of space. Bob had forgotten to tell me that I was supposed to press a button when I wanted to stop and he just let it go faster and faster, to the delight of midfielder Neil Maddison who was stood laughing in the corner while I almost had a coronary.

"I lived to tell the tale, but watching the Juninho game I started to wish I hadn't as it was a massive anti-climax. The match itself was poor and the star refused to do many interviews. It was becoming clear at that time that a move back to Teesside was not on the cards."

Bernie: *"If Juninho had returned a year earlier I think he'd have got more of a hero's welcome but the speculation about him possibly going to Aston Villa and the whole will he, won't he saga was making people a bit fed up.*

"I don't know if he was disinterested or embarrassed but he certainly didn't look like the same wee player and I remember seeing him walk off the park at the end without so much of a wave to the Boro fans.

"It became apparent after that game that Juninho was not set for an immediate return to the Riverside and I have to admit I felt a touch of

*relief as I'd have had to eat a bit of humble pie if he had come back -
and probably custard pie too!"*

Mar 29

The Laws of the game

**Bernie travels to Scunthorpe to interview old team-mate turned
manager Brian Laws. He is a man the Living Legend never really
had in mind as managerial material during their playing days
but, after a lively start which saw Laws sacked for a well
documented bust-up with Italian Ivano Bonetti, he seems to be
enjoying his role at Glanford Park. Seeing another former
colleague involved in the coaching side of the game also gives
Bernie the chance to reflect on the modern game.**

Bernie: *"Lawsy is one that I would never have had down for the
management game. He was a good player with the right attitude but he
was always one of the quieter ones and he kept himself to himself.*

*"But he must have changed because he was sacked from his first
managerial position for throwing a plate of sandwiches or something at
the Italian. That was just one of many funny stories he told me.*

*"Apparently Alex Ferguson was the first person to phone and tell him
not to worry too much after that incident. It was great to see him again
and nice to see he's now doing well at Scunthorpe."*

Gazza and Ali are no April fools

Kind-hearted Boro star Paul Gascoigne goes along to Teesside Hospice to bring a smile to the faces of the youngsters who are sadly poorly enough to be in there. Ali takes the cameras along to film the event and not only is he impressed with the caring attitude of the one and only Gazza, he also has a bit of a brainwave.

Ali: "The Hospice was the football club's chosen charity to support at the time and I knew that the likes of Andy Townsend and Gianluca Festa had also visited previously. Gazza was excellent again that day. There were a lot of people who really wanted to see him and he took time to go round and have a word with or have his picture taken with everyone. It was at that time when it had come out in the press he was playing bingo and the staff at the Hospice were asking him if he'd stay behind and have a game with them!

"At that time, the Hospice were also looking at designing some new fund-raising pin badges and were struggling to come up with ideas. After a bit of thought I suggested...Bernie Lucky Seven Badges. It was just an off-the-cuff idea where Bernie's name and the number he used to play in - seven - could be put on a badge that was designed like a red Boro shirt. Incredibly they liked the idea and from September, everyone will be able to have the Living Legend pinned close to their hearts for just £1."

Bernie: *"When I was a player I always thought visits to hospitals, schools and the like were extremely important things to do. I still get asked to do a lot and in fact, although I wasn't at the hospice with Ali that day, I have visited there recently.*

"It's depressing sometimes when you see people who are poorly but at the same time you know it is something you have to do. If you can help in any way at all, even if it is just bringing a smile to a face for a while, then it's something worth doing.

"For once in his life Ali came up with a fantastic idea and I was more than happy to back it because it is for a very good cause. I hope people will enter into the spirit of things and buy a badge to raise as much cash as possible for the hospice."

Money can't buy success - Blackburn 0 Boro 0

Bernie and Ali head across the Pennines to Ewood Park anticipating a good result against a Blackburn side fighting against relegation. A satisfactory performance sees Boro come home with a valuable draw but one point is less useful for the former Premier League champions.

Ali: "The situation Blackburn were in underlined that throwing money at a football club doesn't necessarily solve problems. The same can be said if you look back to when we had Juninho, Emerson and Ravanelli, yet still got relegated.

"Blackburn had won the title not long before and continued to spend money but it clearly had not worked. They looked totally disjointed against us and it was no surprise to me that they got relegated at the end of the season.

"When we played them it felt strange that the wheel had come full circle since the three points deduction situation a couple of years earlier and that it was them and not us that were in trouble. Oh well, what goes around comes around!"

Bernie: *"There was nothing glamorous about the Blackburn game, it was just a workman-like performance and another good point for Boro. After the game, on the way back to the car, I was talking to Ali about Blackburn striker Ashley Ward and saying how I didn't think he was quite good enough for the Premier League. I continued with this conversation all the way across the Ewood Park car-park, even as we passed a player signing autographs for his adoring fans. I didn't recognise who it was at first but it soon became clear who it was - Ashley Ward! I just hoped he hadn't heard."*

Apr 5

Rampant Ricard - Boro 3 Wimbledon 1

Colombian striker Hamilton Ricard makes it a Happy Easter for Boro fans with a magnificent double strike against The Dons. It's a sign of how he has settled into life and his football on Teesside, less than 12 months after joining his new club. The goals take his tally for the season so far to an impressive 17, but he'll have to go some to reach the target a certain Mr Brownlee set him at the start of the season.

Bernie: *"Hamilton scored two great goals that showed just how instinctive he is. As a striker it was always my philosophy that you should know where the goals are because they never move. If you get a chance you should have a go and that's what Ham did.*

"The double strike took him to an impressive tally but he was still some way off the 60 goals Ali had said he would score - and with games running out I was rubbing my hands together with glee.

"Festa also got on the scoresheet and I was delighted for him because he's a great athlete, a true professional and a class defender. The only problem is sometimes he thinks he's a striker and not a centre-back!"

Ali: "Ham's goals gave me a bit of a sore throat as I went a bit over the top with the commentary as usual. Bernie was getting just as excited as me that day as Boro strolled to an easy win. I kept winding Bernie up by saying Ricard was closing in on the 60-goal target and that all he needed was about ten goals in each of the remaining games!

"Obviously the 60-goal thing was a wind-up that had continued throughout the season and it just showed the entertainment value you can get by saying the odd over-the-top thing on the radio every now and again.

"By that stage I could tell Hamilton was really settled in Middlesbrough and, not only was his form exceptional, but his development as a whole had come on leaps and bounds - in fact his English was already better than Bernie's!"

Apr 7

Ricard goes to pot

The Boro TV cameras make their way to the Riley's snooker club in Middlesbrough to film super striker Hamilton Ricard playing pool. But wires get crossed and instead of an interview with the Colombian star the cameras remain off while Ali and Hamilton battle it out on the green baize - once they've worked out the rules!

Ali: "We arrived at the snooker club ready to interview Ricard and record him playing pool on his own but it immediately became clear that messages had got mixed up and that in fact Big Ham wanted to take me on.

"I reluctantly agreed as Hamilton was cackling away confidently but I was totally baffled as to what he was doing after his first shot as in this country when you play pool you are either pot the spotted balls OR the striped ones.

"Instead he was whacking any old ball around the table seemingly at random. So I stopped him and asked him what was going on, and in his broken English he explained he was potting the balls in numerical order. I realised that he wasn't in fact cheating but simply playing different rules. However, after a bit of explanation we decided to play the Teesside way and he still beat me anyway!"

Apr 8

Home comforts

The local paper on Teesside, the Evening Gazette, do their latest at home with a celebrity feature - at Ali's house! He has no problem in welcoming them into his humble abode but a certain person isn't too happy that he forgot to tidy the place up before the reporter came through the door. The day gets even more exciting when Ali goes to the Tall Trees for a sauna with Bernie.

Ali: "I was happy to let the Gazette into my house and we had a good chat before they went around the place and took a few pictures. Hey presto! I thought nothing more of it until my wife Wendy came in from the shops and started playing hell with me for leaving washing on the line and letting the Rabbit run freely around the garden doing it's dirty business all over the place.

"She was worried it would all show up on the photos in the Gazette and make us look scruffy and I guess she had a point. Luckily I had an excuse to get out of the house as I had an appointment with Slav at the sauna.

"Afterwards Slav and I went into the Tall Trees' Jacuzzi and that's when he sprung a surprise on me. Hiding behind the huge pot plants was Graeme the cameraman and he suddenly came out and presented me with a bottle of champagne.

"It was an early birthday present for me from the Boro TV team but there was a bigger surprise when Bernie grabbed a microphone and began to interview me. It was his revenge for earlier in the season when I had arranged for Gary Gill to interview him."

Bernie: *"Ali had stitched me up with Gary Gill earlier on but I hadn't forgotten and with the season being so long I knew I would get my chance to get him back. It was quality the way it all worked out because not only did I get to interview Ali but the first camera shot captured him opening a bottle of champagne which made him look like a right* *big-time Charlie.*

"We talked about a lot of interesting things like we do in all of the Bernie's Abouts. Many people don't know but Ali has been commentating on Boro for 20-plus years and supporting them for even longer so he does have a lot of good stories.

"He is a complete Boro nut. I'll never forget the first time I walked into his living room and discovered he had pictures of Juninho, Higgy and loads of other Boro lads plastered all over the place.

"It wasn't his birthday until the week after but following the interview we gave him a few early presents - I gave him a pipe and a pair of slippers because he never goes out, and a tub of Slimfast!"

Apr 10

A smokin' good performance - Boro 2 Charlton 0

The Boro bandwagon rolls on as Messrs. Ricard and Mustoe score in a home win against a poor side. It's another important three points and sweet revenge following Charlton's 3-0 win at their place the season before, but there's little for those sat in the commentary box to get excited about apart from remembering the previous match against Charlton.

Ali: "Charlton had always caused us a few problems in the past so it was nice to get one over on them comfortably. They were poor and you could easily see why they were at the wrong end of the table.

"I'll always remember the 3-0 defeat the season before because it was the day one of my then colleagues, Rachel Whatley, thought her cigarette was a microphone believe it or not. After a bit of confusion with the stewards she was placed behind the goal near the travelling Boro fans but she was that stressed she needed a smoke so she lit up. But at that exact point in the commentary I said 'over to our touchline reporter Rachel Whatley' and I caught her that much by surprise that she began talking into her cigarette for a few seconds before embarrassingly realising what she was doing."

Bernie: *"The pressure was on Charlton because they were in danger of going down. I was disappointed because I was used to seeing them play good, entertaining football, but that was far from what we got that day.*

"I remember Charlton manager Alan Curbishley not having much to say after the game and that was totally understandable considering his side's performance. I know how he feels. When one or two of your team don't perform you can still pull through but when all your players have

a bad day you don't have a chance. I've played in games like that where you think everything's going against you and you just can't wait for the final whistle to go."

Apr 13

A dog's life

Throughout his commentating career Ali has always read Boro fanzine Fly Me To The Moon with interest, in particular to see the comic strip character based on the Living Legend and follow the fortunes of Roofus The Boro Dog. So it is no surprise Ali is happy to help launch the 200th edition of FMTTM by writing the foreword.

Ali: "Bernie always features in FMTTM looking like Shaggy out of Scooby Doo. Ever since he was playing I have followed the cartoon and I've always had a laugh at it, even these days when Bernie and I are included.

"I'll always remember the time we helped Craig Hignett try to smuggle his Porsche off a locked car-park at Teesside Airport by lifting up the security barrier but got caught in the act by security. There were only a few of us that knew about that yet it still ended up on the front page of FMTTM, which I found amazing. To this day I still don't know how they found out about it and like all good journalists of course they won't reveal their sources."

Bernie: *"Ali always says my Fly Me To The Moon character looks like Shaggy out of Scooby Doo - and he's absolutely right, although he can't give me too much stick as there's now a cartoon character of him in there as well.*

"It is good because it is light hearted and humorous to read, but that hasn't always been the case. In the past it used to be a wee bit personal because it had a go at some of the players' backgrounds and families. But the modern fanzine is much better."

Apr 14

Ali hits the big 4-0 - Boro 0 Chelsea 0

Boro's arch-rivals Chelsea travel to the Riverside in a bid to make some ground on follow title contenders Manchester United and Arsenal. And on what is Ali's 40th birthday Boro put in an

impressive performance and come close to beating the Blues to give Boro-mad Brownlee a brilliant birthday present.

Bernie: *"Boro played extremely well that night. It was one of the best performances of the season as we stopped an extremely skilful side from playing.*

"For Ali and I football dictates what we do in life so he had to spend his birthday at the BT Cellnet Riverside Stadium. But I'm sure if he's honest he'd say there's no place he'd rather be.

"He loves his job, loves watching the games and loves everything about the club so I know he really enjoyed the night. It's just a shame we didn't come up with a goal as that would have been the perfect birthday present."

Ali: "It was a great performance from Boro and the only disappointment was that, although we deserved it, we didn't win the game. Keith O'Neill really rattled Dennis Wise early on, words were exchanged and that really set the tone for the match. The crowd loved it and it showed that, although the Boro faithful love the silky skills of the likes of Juninho, they also enjoy watching players with fight like O'Neill.

"That night the sound was as loud as I've ever heard it at the Riverside and it was a great way to spend my birthday, although Bernie did give me quite a bit of stick about reaching the big 4-0."

Gibson takes the mike

Club chairman Steve Gibson is the latest man under the spotlight after agreeing to do a Boro TV interview. Bernie is the man asking the questions and Steve, a man who doesn't do too many interviews, is forthcoming with honest answers. It is the latest coup for Boro TV.

Bernie: *"We did a brilliant interview with Steve with one bit filmed at the Riverside and the other at the training ground. It was a nice positive piece looking at everything he's helped achieve in recent years like bringing Robbo and Juninho to the club to other things like the cup final disappointments and much more.*

"Although he shies away from publicity most of the time Steve showed that he is a great talker in front of the camera and that he has a wonderful sense of humour. He came out as the genuine fan that he is.

Many Chairmen act like temperamental superstars but he is a decent bloke who hasn't forgotten his roots and we were proud at Boro TV to be able to give the fans an interview with Steve."

Apr 15

Surprise!

Ali heads to the Purple Onion restaurant in Middlesbrough with his wife Wendy, expecting a quiet family meal to celebrate his birthday. But he's in for something of a shock when he walks in to the bar only to find a huge gathering of family, friends and colleagues, including Bernie, waiting to wish him a happy birthday.

Ali: "Wendy had said we were just going to have a family thing so I walked in to the restaurant completely oblivious that she had something more up her sleeve. I did expect her to have invited one or two of my closer friends but when I walked in and found a room full I was absolutely stuck for words - something I have never ever been before.

"It was a brilliant night because there were people there who I've known for years as well as many friends I've made in recent years through covering the Boro. And of course Bernie was there to eat all the sandwiches and drink all the soft drinks.

"For once Slav brought his lovely wife Karen along for a night out and proved to everyone that he really is married and that she is not a figment of his imagination."

Bernie: *"I'll remember that night for a long time because I have to say it's the only time I've ever seen Ali stuck for words. I'll also never forget some of the old photos of Ali that his wife Wendy had put up in the Purple Onion. There was one of him from years ago when he ran a half marathon. He was built like a beanpole - I don't know what's happened to him since."*

Apr 17

Kinder Surprise - Coventry 1 Boro 2

The good form continues as Boro travel to Highfield Road and pick up three points thanks to goals from Vladimir Kinder and Dean Gordon. All thoughts turn to Slovakian Kinder who has

only featured in three matches, scoring two great goals on the way, and Gordon who doesn't seem to score many but when he does he does it in style.

Bernie: "I'll never know how we won the game because Coventry were excellent in the second half but we hung on in there for what was a great result. Dean Gordon continued to show that he was a bargain buy at under £1 million. Again he scored a cracking goal and the fact that he actually went on to become Boro's only player to play every Premier League game highlights how consistent he is. However I was gutted that Kinder scored as it meant I had to put up with Ali's usual 'Kinder Surprise' comments during the commentary."

Ali: "As members of the press we all remembered Gordon Strachan's strange press conference at the Riverside and wondered what comments he would come out with this time if we won.

"There was also a bizarre spell after Gary Pallister clashed with their goalkeeper Magnus Hedman. Strachan refused to take Hedman off, and when Kinder hit his goal it did seem that the 'keeper was struggling badly to get to it because he was still injured.

"Kinder's goal was just a reminder to everyone of the way he can play but how he had not fulfilled his potential and never really got in the side consistently. Gordon's goal was another peach and he proved yet again that if he scores he does it with a bang."

Apr 20

Page is booked

Boro's matchday announcer and former Radio One DJ Mark Page is the latest person the Boro TV cameras turn to. He is a man Ali knows well through the media but the connections go back further as the pair were in the same school class as each other along with another locally born celebrity.

Ali: "The thing about Mark Page is that he always makes out that he's in his thirties but he went to school with me so I can exclusively reveal that he's exactly the same age as me.

"In fact we were in the same class at King's Manor school in Middlesbrough, along with Bob Mortimer of Vic and Bob fame. What a classroom that must have been - I'll bet we were a nightmare for the teacher! Pagey certainly had the gift of the gab even in those days and he used to tell everyone how he was going to score a hat-trick for the school team, even though he never managed to do so.

"The best story about Mark Page I can remember comes from the time he was out in Cyprus to play against an Armed Forces side with Steve Gibson and some lads from Bulkhaul when a few soldiers decided to have a laugh at his expense.

"The team had just sat down for their evening meal when two burly squaddies burst into the room, lifted up Pagey's chair with him sat in it, and carried him away kicking and screaming before throwing him into the sea fully clothed. I find it a bit strange that it's a tale he's never recounted in his 'Me Mark Page' column in the Evening Gazette."

Apr 24

What a balls up! - Boro 1 Arsenal 6

The arrival of the Gunners is eagerly anticipated as they have had a great season and are pushing for the Premier League title. And in a game that really is men and against boys, they prove exactly why they are going for the silverware by inflicting Boro's worst home defeat of the season. But it is not the only thing that goes wrong that day for Ali.

Ali: "One of my boss's business colleagues is a keen Arsenal fan and he'd asked me to get a football signed for him by all his heroes. I went out and bought a ball and got permission to put it, along with a permanent marker, in the away dressing room for the Gunners to sign when they arrived. I left it there and went back up to the press box to commentate on the game.

"In terms of atmosphere it was one of the best I've heard at the Riverside, despite the appalling result. I was gutted when we got thrashed but I kept thinking that at least I was getting in the boss's good books - that is until I went back to the changing room and found the ball had disappeared!

"It later turned out that the Arsenal lads had in fact signed the ball, but then picked it up and taken it back to London with them. Despite several phone calls to Highbury since I still haven't got my hands on it. So, if you're reading this Mr Wenger..."

Bernie: *"Arsenal had the passing, movement, pace, finishing - everything really. We just weren't at the races. I've been on the wrong end of thrashings myself and I know exactly how it feels. It is degrading and when you are part of a game like that you just want* the final whistle to go. Of course there's also the matches where you win by a big margin, and those are games that you want to last forever.

"But I must say the fans were excellent even though they must have been sick as parrots. There was a lot of good banter between both sets of supporters. At the end of the day all anyone could really do was take their hats off to Arsenal.

"On the other side of things it was also a very positive day for Alun Armstrong. After all his injury problems it must have been nice to come on and score his first ever Premier League goal against a defence which is one of the best in the country."

Apr 30

Best of friends

Bernie travels to Doncaster for a chat with former Boro striker Paul Wilkinson. The pair played together at Ayresome Park but, despite playing in the same position and on certain occasions keeping each other out of the starting line-up, they have remained friends.

Bernie: "Wilko is a good lad, there's no doubt about that. Throughout my career some people have thought there was a problem between us but that is absolute nonsense. He is a quiet, family-man type who wouldn't harm a fly and we used to get on well. And the thing is that if someone took my place I would never go to that player if I had a complaint because he didn't pick the team, the manager does that.

"We had an interesting chat with Wilko who was playing for Northampton at the time. Funnily enough they were relegated to Division Three a couple of weeks later - the Slaven curse strikes again!"

May 3

Howzat!

For almost a year Ali and Boro's Aussie goalkeeper Mark Schwarzer have been at loggerheads as to whose country rules supreme - at cricket. So the pair get together for a game themselves and then when the Cricket World Cup comes around and Australia look destined to be knocked out of the tournament by South Africa Ali decides to get one over on Big Schwarz, well in theory anyway!

Ali: "During the season Schwarz and I had had this raging battle and the odd flutter along the way as to who was better at cricket - England or Australia. With the World Cup approaching, we decided to face each other in front of the cameras at Saltburn Cricket Club. We were the only players on the pitch apart from a stunned passer-by who we grabbed as a fielder, and we both wore our country's colours.

"We had an umpire called Maurice who I think last officiated a match in about 1922. He wandered around in his white coat and kept saying that in all the games he's umpired over the years he's never given anyone out lbw.

"We bowled two overs at each other and much to Schwarzer's delight he beat me by a couple of runs. I knew I was in for some stick over the next season from the Big Aussie but just a couple of weeks later during the World Cup I could smell revenge.

"Schwarzer was enjoying a holiday in Spain unaware that his side were about to get knocked out of the tournament by South Africa - that is until I rang him on his mobile to talk him through it.

"Then the game took an unbelievable twist as South Africa's Allan Donald was dramatically run out - handing the Aussies victory with the very last ball of the game. The delirious shouts that came sounding out from the Costa Del Sol are still ringing in my ears to this day, and once more Schwarzer had got one over on me."

May 4

The worst day of my life

Sometimes in this life you have to confront your fears and that is exactly what Ali had to do in his pursuit of an interview with Boro new boy Keith O'Neill. Game-for-a-laugh Keith is certainly not the kind of individual you would sit and interview in a quiet

restaurant so it is decided that on a moving rollercoaster is the ideal place. But there's just one problem - Mr Brownlee's worst fear is rollercoasters!

Ali: "I have been to theme parks on many an occasion with my family but I've never been anywhere near a rollercoaster because they absolutely scare me to death. So when our producer told me I was going to interview Keith on a rollercoaster at Lightwater Valley you can imagine what my reaction was! I reluctantly agreed to do it but my nerves were even more shredded when I was told that the ride is in fact the longest rollercoaster in the world.

"We arrived on the day and Keith was well up for it. In fact his key phrase for the day was 'Boro TV, they're madder than me'. But I'm not so sure that's true. Keith was great company and excellent to interview and that took my mind off things a bit - at least until the ride started. If we'd only been on the thing once I might have been alright but by the time the cameraman had got all his shots right I'd been round the damn thing five times and was as white as a ghost!"

Bernie: *"Ali never let us know until the last minute that he was scared to death of rollercoasters so we just went ahead with our plans. It turned into a really good interview because Keith is definitely game for a laugh. The only thing that surprised me is that they both managed to get into the same carriage - what with Ali's fine physique and all! Keith is a wacky character so if we had just sat him down in a room and stuck a camera in his face it wouldn't have worked as well. It was right up his street."*

Karaoke time

Once Ali has overcome his worst fear he rushes back to Teesside as he is due at the Middlesbrough Official Supporters' Club Player of the Year Awards at the BT Cellnet Riverside Stadium. The night is a great success as Hamilton Ricard and Robbie Stockdale are presented with their Player of the Year and Young Player of the Year awards respectively. If only Ali could sing as well as those two can play football.

Ali: "It was great to see Hamilton scoop an award that he really deserved. He confidently stood up in front of everyone and gave a speech which showed just how much his English had come on in the space of a year or so.

"Then the disco kicked in, closely followed by the karaoke. Over the years that part of the evening has become a bit of a loose cannon as we've had young Boro star Anthony Ormerod singing 'Crocodile Rock' and perhaps even more famously, Dave Allan, the club's PR manager, with his own version of 'Cheer Up Peter Reid'.

"So this time around it was my turn to take to the stage, this time with two different members of the club's PR team, Chris Kershaw and Louise Wanless, to attempt to sing 'Hi Ho Silver Lining'.

"I don't know quite how good my vocal chords sounded but Chris can't have done too badly because he met his girlfriend Lucy for the first time that evening and she clearly wasn't put off by his singing!"

May 5

Robbo's all at sea

The final Bernie's About of the season is set to be filmed and Bryan Robson is chosen as the interviewee. It is decided to do the piece in style and Boro TV do just that as Robbo joins the Living Legend on a yacht in Hartlepool Marina. However the Boro boss takes to the sailing game a little better than Bernie, who proves that it's not just aeroplanes he's not so keen on.

Bernie: "Following our chat with Keith O'Neill on the rollercoaster we decided it was important to do something different with Robbo, so we took him sailing at Hartlepool.

"We arrived at the marina and I had one cup of tea that I thought may as well have been sea water it was that awful. However Robbo was downing it like it was going out of fashion - he must have thought it was Earl Grey!

"We boarded the yacht and had a chat off the record before beginning the interview. Robbo was in great spirits and we did a brilliant piece with him. He talked all about a lot of things including how he's now moved to the Teesside area - which is something a lot of the fans have been wanting to ask him about for a while. It was the ideal way to finish off a season of Bernie's Abouts. The only problem was that we didn't actually get out to sea. The water was too choppy that day so we spent the next few hours sailing round and round the marina!"

Ali: "We originally thought about taking the boss to a nice restaurant but when he heard about this he asked if there was anything more exciting we could do - obviously he'd heard about us taking Keith O'Neill on the rollercoaster.

"We all put our thinking caps on and it wasn't until my phone-in sidekick Bob Moncur, who incidentally is Robbo's boyhood hero, told me that his friend had a yacht that we knew we had found the perfect place for the interview.

"As always Robbo was happy to talk to us and he looked comfortable in the surroundings of the North Sea - a lot more so than the Living Legend it has to be said who showed that it's not just planes that make him feel queasy."

May 8

Bob's the word - Boro 0 Manchester Utd 1

Title contenders Manchester United travel to the Riverside looking for three points in their push for the Premiership, but also with the aim of avenging the 3-2 defeat Boro inflicted on them in the game at Old Trafford. The game is won by a solitary Dwight Yorke goal for the visitors but the day could be an interesting one for Ali, who hopes to meet up with an old school-mate.

Ali: "I was really looking forward to the Man Utd game for two reasons - firstly I couldn't wait for us to give them a good beating like we did and secondly there was a chance I would meet up with my old school-mate Bob Mortimer.

"Unfortunately neither of my wishes came true. United got their revenge by beating us 1-0 and both Bob - who is Boro's famous fan representative in the Premier League Hall of Fame - and I were too busy doing our own things to get together for a chat."

Bernie: *"The game was a bit of a damp squib, certainly not the classic a lot of people expected. It has to be said that on the day Man Utd deserved it. They are a quality side as they proved by going on and doing the treble.*

"People were tipping us to beat them because we had done so at Old Trafford but it would take a very good side to beat them twice, and on the day they showed they are a class outfit.

"When we won at their place in December it woke them up and they went on a very good run on the way to the title. But it's nice to be able to say that we were the last team to beat them at Old Trafford in what was such a historic season for them. And of course it meant there was no danger of me having to show my bum!"

I'm forever blowing bubbles - West Ham 4 Boro 0

Boro's first season back in the top flight ends with a trip to Upton Park to take on West Ham. The side don't exactly go out in style but the result means they finish ninth in the Premier League and Boro's travelling army of fans enjoy the occasion despite the result and one or two other strange goings on in the capital.

Bernie: *"It was a strange day at Upton Park, not only because of the result, but because we walked right into the middle of a world record attempt - for blowing the most bubbles. It was great for me because I took the opportunity to nab all the bottles of bubbles that had been left under the seats for all the press to take home for my kids, so that was half the record gone!*

"I remember the travelling Boro fans being excellent that day, as they always are. Many of them were in fancy dress. One young lady was dressed as a French maid and her outfit was that skimpy that it must have distracted half of the players - hence the result.

"On the pitch it was a poor showing. It was a typical end of season game where there was nothing to play for other than pride but there were a few non-performers in the Boro side that day. It was a shame for the supporters who had travelled all that way hoping to finish the season in style."

Ali: "We were all really looking forward to the last game followed by a well deserved rest during the closed season. But what we thought would be a run-of-the-mill final game in fact turned out to be quite a strange occasion.

"When we got there we were told that the club was trying to blow the world record number of bubbles. We had no idea what they were talking about until we found plastic bottles of liquid on our seats in the press box.

"The idea was that we were supposed to partake in a mass bubble-blowing exercise with the fans but my sidekick Mr Slaven chose instead to fill his bag with the bottles whilst muttering the words 'these will make perfect Christmas presents'.

"Even weirder were these four blokes who stood on the four corners of the pitch modelling West Ham's new kit but the funny thing was that they had no shirts on, instead they had paint-on kits on their top halves. It was a strange day all round and to make matters worse we were trounced. But the away fans were magnificent with their support, despite the scoreline, and they summed up just how good a season it had been for Boro."

May 21

Face to face with Lennie

The last interview of the season sees the Living Legend come face to face with his old gaffer Lennie Lawrence. It has been well documented that the pair weren't always on the best of terms during their time at the Boro but it is time for any grudges to be forgotten as Bernie poses the questions to the Luton manager.

Bernie: "Throughout the season Ali had been trying to get Lennie to do an interview. At first I told him he must be joking if he thought I was asking him the questions, but then I realised there is no point in holding any grudges.

"I'm on another side of the business now and it's important that I'm professional about it. Ali mentioned to me that Gary Lineker had fallen out with Graham Taylor in their England days together, yet he'd since made up and interviewed him. That's when I knew I had to chat with Lennie.

"When Lennie first walked in I said 'I can't believe I'm going to be talking to you' and he just laughed. That was the ice broken right away and after a chat off-camera we got down to the real thing.

"We had a right few goes at each other when we were at Boro together and we didn't leave on good terms so sitting down and talking like adults did seem a bit strange. But he spoke well and yet again it resulted in another excellent Boro TV interview."

Ali: "There was always the danger that it might turn into a slanging match and that is something no-one would like to see. Bernie had made his views on Lennie very clear in the past and I just wondered whether, with his fiery temper, he might lose it a bit. So there was a bit of trepidation when we went into the interview. But things went very well, we got a good interview and whilst I wouldn't say they are now the greatest of friends, I think it went some way towards helping the healing process."

May 27

They think it's all over...it is now

Following his rear-ly impressive show in Binn's shop window earlier in the season Bernie receives a call asking him to appear on popular BBC sports quiz They Think It's All Over, and to bare his backside once more as part of the 'feel a sports personality' round. Reluctantly he agrees and once at the studio in London he not only finds himself amongst familiar faces but also becomes the star of the show.

Bernie: "I wasn't really nervous for my big appearance because of all the practice I've had on Boro TV, but I still rehearsed the lifting of my kilt in the dressing room mirror a few times before the big moment.

"When I walked onto the set I walked past a blindfolded Jonathan Ross and I couldn't resist having a playful grab of his crown jewels. He seemed to quite enjoy that and from that moment on he thought the mystery guest was a woman - much to his dismay when he actually found out it was me!

"Then I saw Gary McAllister sat there as one of the guest panelists. I know Gary from when I was playing at Albion Rovers and he was at Motherwell and as soon as we saw each other we were both killing ourselves laughing.

"I was facing the teams with my bum on show to the audience - and the whole nation! - and I could also see Gary Lineker laughing. The whole thing was hilarious although I have to admit to being a bit worried when Jonathan Ross said to me 'I hope you enjoyed that as much as I did'.

"After the show Nick Hancock and everyone else joined us for a drink. I had a good chat with McAllister to catch up on the old times. It was a great day all round."

Into the Millennium

With another exhausting season over, Bernie and Ali get themselves a well deserved break. But with every passing day the new season - one that will take Boro into the new Millennium - gets ever closer and there is little time to reflect as thoughts turn to the resumption of football and what the future may hold.

Ali: "Once the season was over I think I breathed a sigh of relief, not only because Boro had done so well in retaining Premier League status but also because everything else had also progressed at such a rapid rate.

"It was our first full season on Boro TV, and a very successful one at that, and I also felt our Century Radio commentaries came on leaps and bounds as well. Many people refer to Bernie and I as a double act and over the year I began to see what they meant as our working relationship improved.

"But as is always the case with football the new season is always around the corner and so we turn our attentions to the next season. Hopefully it is one in which we can build on what we have achieved and march towards that first major honour.

"Plans are well in place to make Boro TV and Century Radio much bigger and better so unless Bernie continues to go around showing his bum in shop windows and gets us the sack we'll hopefully be around for some time yet."

Bernie: *"On the pitch it was a very hard-working season for the Boro lads and although it wasn't entertaining a lot of the time they gave their all and consolidated their place in the Premier League.*

"From a personal point of view I also feel I became more confident as a TV and radio presenter over the course of the year. A couple of years ago when I started I was tentative and didn't say as much - now I say what I like!

"I have made a decision that I want to carry on working on this side of things and continue working with the Boro. I'm a fan, I live here and I'm happy in what I'm doing. Things are progressing and developing all the time and I want to be a part of it.

"The only worry I have now is what I'll do on the long trips to away games this season. Our radio colleague Rachel has moved on to pastures new so I won't be able to rest my head in her bosom - then again there's always Ali!"